Healing Verses of the Holy Qur'an & Hadith

Healing Verses of the Holy Qur'an & Hadith

Shaykh Muhammad Hisham Kabbani

PUBLISHED BY THE
INSTITUTE FOR SPIRITUAL AND CULTURAL ADVANCEMENT

Published and Distributed by:

Institute for Spiritual and Cultural Advancement (ISCA)
17195 Silver Parkway, #201
Fenton, MI 48430 USA
Tel: (888) 278-6624
Fax: (810) 815-0518
Email: staff@naqshbandi.org
Web: http://www.naqshbandi.org

First Edition: December 2013
Healing Verses of the Holy Qur'an and Hadith
ISBN: 978-1-938058-12-7

PRINTED IN THE UNITED STATES OF AMERICA
15 14 13 12 11 05 06 07 08 09

The author with his beloved master, His Eminence, Shaykh Muhammad Nazim Adil al-Haqqani. Cyprus, Sept. 2013.

Shaykh Kabbani giving a *suhbah*, an inspired spiritual discourse, in the renowned Naqshbandi *zawiya* in Michigan. In 1990, after thirty years of training he was authorized by his master to teach Islamic spirituality (*tasawwuf*). July 2013.

Table of Contents

About the Author i

Preface iii

Publisher's Notes v

Masters of the Naqshbandi-Haqqani Golden Chain ix

Recitation before Every Association xi

Verses of Holy Qur'an Heal and the Wisdom is to Ask 1

Allah Wants Us to be Persistent in Our Du`a 9

Three Levels of Du`a for Three Levels of Affliction 13

Allah Wants You to Persist in Asking Him 17

Consistent Du`a is Better than Tricks of Charlatans 19

Conditions of Du`a and How to Perfect It 27

How to Perfect Your Du`a 29

What Prevents Du`a from Being Accepted 31

Conditions for Du`a to be Accepted 33

The Best Times to Make Du`a and Fulfilling what is Prescribed 35

The Importance of Giving Charity to Secure Your Du`a 39

Special Healing Supplications with Allah's Name 45

The Du`a with Ismullahi 'l-`Azham is Like a Sword 46

The Supplication of Sayyidina Yunus 51

Mercy and Healing for Those Who Read Holy Qur'an 52

Holy Qur'an is the Only Book that Gives and Does Not Take 57

Supplication for Calamity and the Adab of Du`a 61

Shaytan Enters a Weak Area and Brings Disease 62

Blocking the Weak Entry Point 63

From Sayyidina al-Hasan, Du`a of the Sahaabi 65

Supplicate in Places Where it is Accepted 69

Du`a of the Sahaabi Saved from Murder 71

Reading Holy Qur'an is Salvation from Punishment and the Path to Mercy 79
Shaykhs of Tariqah That Keep Shari`ah 81
Professional Shaykhs 82
The Charlatans 82
Real Martyrdom 91
Those Whom Allah Will Deem Liars and Throw in Hell 92
Sayyidina Ali Defines True Martyrdom 96
Stunning Examples of the Sahaabah 105
The Wisdom of Avoiding Long-Term Planning 106
Amazing Sayings of the Sahaabah 115
Islamic Calendar and Holy Days 125
Glossary 129
Other Publications 134

About the Author

World-renowned religious scholar Shaykh Muhammad Hisham Kabbani is featured in the ground-breaking book published by Georgetown University, *The 500 Most Influential Muslims in the World*. For decades, he has promoted traditional Islamic principles of peace, tolerance, love, compassion and brotherhood, while rigorously opposing extremism in all its forms. He hails from a respected family of traditional Islamic scholars, which includes the former head of the Association of Muslim Scholars of Lebanon and the present grand mufti (highest Islamic religious authority) of Lebanon.

Shaykh Kabbani is highly trained, both as a western scientist and as an Islamic scholar. He received a Bachelor's degree in Chemistry and later studied medicine. Under the instruction of Shaykh 'AbdAllāh ad-Daghestani of Damascus, he holds a degree in Islamic Divine Law. Shaykh Muhammad Nazim Adil al-Haqqani, world leader of the Naqshbandi-Haqqani Sufi Order, authorized him to teach and counsel students in Sufism.

In his long-standing effort to promote a better understanding of traditional Islam, in February 2010, Shaykh Kabbani hosted HRH Charles, the Prince of Wales at a cultural event at the revered Old Trafford Stadium in Manchester, U.K. He has hosted two international conferences in the U.S., and regional conferences on a host of contemporary issues that attracted moderate Muslim scholars from Asia, the Far East, Middle East, Africa, U.K. and Eastern Europe. His counsel is sought by media outlets academics, policymakers and government leaders.

For thirty years, Shaykh Kabbani has consistently promoted peaceful cooperation among people of all beliefs. Since the early 1990s, he launched numerous endeavors to bring moderate Muslims into the mainstream. Often at great personal risk, he has been instrumental in awakening Muslim social consciousness regarding the religious duty to stand firm against extremism and terrorism, for the benefit of all. His bright, hopeful outlook, with a goal to honor and serve all humanity, has helped millions understand the difference between moderate mainstream Muslims and minority extremist sects.

In the United States, Shaykh Kabbani serves as Chairman, Islamic Supreme Council of America; Founder, Naqshbandi Sufi Order of America; Advisor, World Organization for Resource Development and Education; Chairman, As-*Sunnah* Foundation of America; Founder, *The Muslim Magazine*. In the United Kingdom, Shaykh Kabbani is an advisor to Sufi Muslim Council, which consults to the British government on public policy and social and religious issues.

Other titles by Shaykh Kabbani include: *The Benefits of Bismillah 'ir-Rahman 'ir-Raheem & Surat al-Fatihah* (2013), *The Importance of Prophet Muhammad in Our Daily Life* (2013), *The Hierarchy of Saints* (2013), *The Dome of Provisions* (2012), *Salawat of Tremendous Blessings* (2012, also in Turkish/Spanish), *The Heavenly Power of Divine Obedience and Gratitude* (2012), *The Sufilive Series* (2010-2012), *At the Feet of My Master* (2010, 2 vols.), *The Nine-fold Ascent* (2009), *Banquet for the Soul* (2008), *Illuminations* (2007), *Universe Rising* (2007), *Symphony of Remembrance* (2007), *A Spiritual Commentary on the Chapter of Sincerity* (2006), *The Sufi Science of Self-Realization* (Fons Vitae, 2005), *Keys to the Divine Kingdom* (2005), *Classical Islam and the Naqshbandi Sufi Order* (2004), *The Naqshbandi Sufi Tradition Guidebook* (2004), *The Approach of Armageddon? An Islamic Perspective* (2003), *Encyclopedia of Muhammad's Women Companions and the Traditions They Related* (1998, with Dr. Laleh Bakhtiar), *Encyclopedia of Islamic Doctrine* (7 vols. 1998), *Angels Unveiled* (1996), *The Naqshbandi Sufi Way* (1995), and *Remembrance of God Liturgy of the Sufi Naqshbandi Masters* (1994).

Preface

Healing Verses in the Holy Qur'an and Hadith* is based on the extemporaneous, divinely inspired discourses (*suhbah*) of Shaykh Hisham Kabbani, disciple and representative of the global head of the Naqshbandi-Haqqani Sufi Order, Shaykh Muhammad Nazim Adil al-Haqqani. Their uplifting discourses often include anecdotes of venerable Sufi masters from the renowned Naqshbandi Golden Chain, which dates back to Prophet Muhammad (may the peace and blessing of God be forever upon him).

In addition to citing Holy Qur'an and Hadith, this work presents detailed explanations from pre-eminent scholarly works, including: *Sahih Bukhari, Sahih Muslim; Sahih Ibn al-Habban* and *Sunan Tirmidhi*; Bukhari's *Adab al-Mufrad (Etiquette of Personal Ethics);* Imam Ahmad's *Musnad (Reliable Hadith);* \`Abdullah ibn Ahmad ibn Hanbal's *Kitaab al-Zuhd (Book of Asceticism); Al-Jawaab al-Kaafee liman sa'ala \`ala ad-daw\`a ish-shafi\`i (The Sufficient Answers for Those Who Asked about the Healing Medicine)* and *Madarij as-Salikeen (Stations of the Travelers on the Path)*, each by Ibn Qayyim al-Jawziyya; and, Ibn Abi ad-Dunya's *Kitab al-Mujabeen (Book of Those Whose Du\`as Allah Accepted).*

Healing Verses in the Holy Qur'an and Hadith includes several powerful supplications taught by Prophet Muhammad and their secret spiritual knowledge that is hidden in specific formulas handed down over centuries that are known to remove obstacles, resolve poor health, financial and personal issues, impart goodness and bring peace to one's heart.

These universal lessons are a fine addition to any study of Islam, Prophet Muhammad, Sufism, Islamic mysticism, spirituality and New Age teachings.

For fifty years, the author has sought to serve his master and promote these ancient Sufi teachings in the best manner. We hope the book you now hold reflects this spirit and opens a door to the spiritual healing found in the Holy Qur'an and Hadith.

Publisher's Notes

This book is directed to those familiar with the Sufi Way; however, to accommodate lay readers unfamiliar with Sufi terminology and practices, we have provided English translations of Arabic texts and a comprehensive glossary. Where Arabic terms are crucial to the discussion, we have included transliteration and explanations. For readers familiar with Arabic and Islamic teachings, for further clarity please consult the cited sources.

The original material is based on transcripts of a series of holy gatherings known as *ṣuḥbah,* a divinely inspired talk given by the "Shaykh," a highly trained spiritual guide. To present the authentic flavor of such rare teachings, great care was taken to preserve the speaking styles of both the author and the illustrious shaykhs upon whose notes this book is based.

Translations from Arabic to English pose unique challenges that we have tried our best to make understandable to Western readers. Please note our application of the common Arabic oral tradition of omitting definite articles such as "the Prophet" and "the Holy Qur'an," as practiced by Muslims around the world as intimate references.

We apply contemporary American English publishing standards and italicize foreign proper nouns (*Fātiḥah, Quṭb az-Zamān, Rasūlullāh, Sūratu 'n-Naml),* but not commonly known foreign-language nouns (jihād, Qur'an, shaykh) unless they appear in transliterations.

Quotes from the Holy Qur'an and Holy Traditions of Prophet Muhammad are offset, italicized and cited.

The pronoun "they" is frequently used by Sufi guides to reference heavenly beings and holy souls who support them and give them orders, a usage that appears throughout this book. Where gender-specific pronouns such as "he" and "him" are applied in a general sense, no discrimination is intended towards women, upon whom The Almighty bestowed great honor.

Islamic teachings are primarily based on four sources, in this order:

- **Holy Qur'an**: the Islamic holy book of divine revelation (God's Word) granted to Prophet Muhammad. Reference to Holy Qur'an appears as "4:12," which indicates "Chapter 4, Verse 12."
- ***Sunnah***: holy traditions of Prophet Muhammad ﷺ; the systematic recording of his words and actions that comprise the *ḥadīth.* For fifteen

centuries, Islam has applied a strict, highly technical standard, rating each narration in terms of its authenticity and categorizing its "transmission." As this book is not highly technical, we simplified the reporting of *ḥadīth,* but included the narrator and source texts to support the discussion at hand.

- ***Ijma*'**: The adherence, or agreement of the experts of independent reasoning *(āhl al-ijtihād)* to the conclusions of a given ruling pertaining to what is permitted and what is forbidden after the passing of the Prophet, Peace be upon him, as well as the agreement of the Community of Muslims concerning what is obligatorily known of the religion with its decisive proofs. Perhaps a clearer statement of this principle is, "We do not separate (in belief and practice) from the largest group of the Muslims."
- **Legal Rulings:** highly trained Islamic scholars form legal rulings from their interpretation of the Qur'an and the *Sunnah,* known as *ijtihād.* Such rulings are intended to provide Muslims an Islamic context regarding contemporary social norms. In theological terms, scholars who form legal opinions have completed many years of rigorous training and possess degrees similar to a doctorate in divinity in Islamic knowledge, or in legal terms, hold the status of a high court or supreme court judge, or higher.

The following universally recognized symbols have been respectfully included in this work and are deeply appreciated by a vast majority of our readers.

ﷻ *Subḥānahu wa Taʿalā* (may His Glory be Exalted), recited after the name "Allāh" and any of the Islamic names of God.

ﷺ *ṢallAllāhu ʿalayhi wa sallam* (God's blessings and greetings of peace be upon him), recited after the holy name of Prophet Muhammad.

ؑ *ʿAlayhi ʿs-salām* (peace be upon him/her), recited after holy names of other prophets, names of Prophet Muhammad's relatives, the pure and virtuous women in Islam, and angels.

ؓ/ؓ *RaḍīAllāhu ʿanh(um)* (may God be pleased with him/her), recited after the holy names of Companions of Prophet Muhammad; plural: *raḍīAllāhu ʿanhum.*

ق represents *QaddasAllāhu sirrah* (may God sanctify his secret), recited after names of saints.

Transliteration

Transliteration from Arabic to English poses challenges. To show respect, Muslims often capitalize nouns which, in English, appear in lowercase.

To facilitate authentic pronunciation of names, places and terms, use the following key:

Symbol	Transliteration	Symbol	Transliteration	Vowels: Long	
ء	ʼ	ط	ṭ	آ ى	ā
ب	b	ظ	ẓ	و	ū
ت	t	ع	ʻ	ي	ī
ث	th	غ	gh	**Short**	
ج	j	ف	f	َ	a
ح	ḥ	ق	q	ُ	u
خ	kh	ك	k	ِ	i
د	d	ل	l		
ذ	dh	م	m		
ر	r	ن	n		
ز	z	ه	h		
س	s	و	w		
ش	sh	ي	y		
ص	ṣ	ة	ah; at		
ض	ḍ	ال	al-/'l-		

Masters of the Naqshbandi-Haqqani Golden Chain

May Allah ﷻ preserve their secrets.

1. Prophet Muhammad ibn ʿAbdAllah ﷺ

2. Abū Bakr as-Ṣiddīq ق
3. Salmān al-Farsi ق
4. Qasim bin Muhammad bin Abū Bakr ق
5. Jafar aṣ-Ṣādiq ق
6. Tayfur Abū Yazīd al-Bistāmi ق
7. AbūlHassan ʿAlī al-Kharqani ق
8. Abū ʿAlī al-Farmadi ق
9. Abū Yaqūb Yusuf al-Hamadani ق
10. AbūlAbbas, al-Khiḍr ق
11. ʿAbdul Khāliq al-Ghujdawani ق
12. Arif ar-Riwakri ق
13. Khwaja Maḥmūd al-Anjir al-Faghnawi ق
14. ʿAlī ar-Ramitani ق
15. Muhammad Baba as-Samasi ق
16. as-Sayyid Amir Kulal ق
17. Muhammad Bahaʿuddin Shah Naqshband ق
18. Alaʿuddin al-Bukhāri al-Attar ق
19. Yaqūb al-Charkhi ق
20. Ubaydullāh al-Aḥrar ق
21. Muhammad az-Zahid ق
22. Darwish Muhammad ق
23. Muhammad Khwaja al-Amkanaki ق
24. Muhammad al-Baqi billāh ق
25. Aḥmad al-Farūqi as-Sirhindi ق
26. Muhammad al-Masum ق
27. Muhammad Sayfuddin al-Farūqi al-Mujaddidi ق
28. as-Sayyid Nūr Muhammad al-Badawani ق
29. Shamsuddin Habib Allah ق
30. ʿAbdAllah ad-Dahlawi ق
31. Khālid al-Baghdādī ق
32. Ismail Muhammad ash-Shirwāni ق
33. Khas Muhammad Shirwāni ق
34. Muhammad Effendi al-Yaraghi ق
35. Jamāluddin al-Ghumuqi al-Ḥusayni ق
36. Abū Aḥmad as-Sughuri ق
37. Abū Muhammad al-Madani ق
38. Sharafuddīn ad-Daghestāni ق
39. ʿAbdAllah al-Faʿiz ad-Daghestāni
40. Muhammad Nazim Adil al-Haqqaniق

Recitation before Every Association

A'ūdhu billāhi min ash-Shayṭān ir-rajīm.
Bismillāhi' r-Raḥmāni 'r-Raḥīm.
Nawaytu 'l-arbā'īn, nawaytu 'l-'itikāf,
nawaytu'l-khalwah, nawaytu 'l-'uzlah,
nawaytu 'r-riyāḍa, nawaytu 's-sulūk,
lillāhi Ta'alā fī hādhā 'l-masjid.

Ati'ūllāha wa ati' ūr-Rasūla
wa ūli'l-amri minkum.

I seek refuge in Allah from Satan, the rejected.
In the Name of Allah, the Merciful,
the Compassionate.
I intend the forty (days of seclusion);
I intend seclusion in the mosque,
I intend seclusion, I intend isolation,
I intend discipline (of the ego); I intend to travel
in God's Path for the sake of God,
in this mosque.

Obey Allah, obey the Prophet,
and obey those in authority among you.

Sūratu 'n-Nisā (The Women), 4:59

Verses of Holy Qur'an Heal and the Wisdom is to Ask

A'ūdhu billāhi min ash-Shayṭāni 'r-rajīm. Bismillāhi' r-Raḥmāni 'r-Raḥīm. Nawaytu 'l-arbā'īn, nawaytu 'l-'itikāf, nawaytu'l-khalwah, nawaytu 'l-'uzlah, nawaytu 'r-riyāḍa, nawaytu 's-sulūk, lillāhi Ta'alā fī hādhā 'l-masjid. Atī'ūllāha wa atī'ū 'r-Rasūla wa ūlī 'l-amri minkum. Obey Allah, obey the Prophet, and obey those in authority among you. (4:59)

Dastūr, madad yā Sulṭān al-Awlīyā, Mawlana Shaykh Nazim al-Haqqani ق.
Dastūr, madad yā Sulṭān al-Awlīyā, Mawlana Shaykh 'AbdAllah ad-Daghestani ق.

Every one of us around the world, in general, Muslim and non-Muslim, have something in common: everyone is trying to eliminate as much as possible from this problem that is facing everyone, that comes on all of us without distinguishing the child, adult, young and old, at any time in our lives. People only have a basic understanding that this is a common issue, but they cannot determine when it comes and when it goes. When it comes, it comes suddenly and when it goes, it goes slowly and then disappears. So all people share this issue of sickness, from the time of Sayyidina Adam ﷺ up to today and until Judgment Day.

Sickness hits everyone; there is not a single person safe from either physical or spiritual sickness and both require an expert to eliminate it from the person under its influence, who tries to lower it as much as possible. Many people recover from physical sickness and some might not recover. Similarly, regarding spiritual sickness that concerns the soul, some people might recover from it and some might not.

Which is more difficult, physical sickness or spiritual sickness? Spiritual sickness is more difficult to treat and not everyone can be cured from it. On the other hand, physical sickness might look more difficult and in reality many get cured from it, although some cannot. So in that case, for physical sickness people must go to a wise person, if you want to call him a doctor, and for spiritual sickness you might call him a guide, in order to try to eliminate as much as possible.

If someone comes to you with his story about his sickness, what do you want to do? For us and most people, they don't go that route, they go a different route, but really if we are *mu'min* and believe in Allah ﷻ and His Prophet ﷺ we go the route that Holy Qur'an and the Hadith of the Prophet ﷺ has encouraged us.

The Prophet ﷺ said:

ما أنزل الله مِنْ داءٍ إلا أنْزَلَ لهُ شِفَاءً

Maa anzal-Allahu min daa'in illa anzala lahu shifaa'an.

Allah did not send a sickness except He sent with it a cure.

(Abu Hurayrah in Sahih Bukhari)

So if we believe in that, then the responsibility of curing is with the One Who Cures, which is Allah ﷻ. So Allah ﷻ will send you a cure if you really believe in what He or the Prophet ﷺ said, and the Prophet ﷺ said, "Allah did not send a sickness except He sent with it a cure."

And Allah ﷻ said in the Holy Qur'an:

يَا أَيُّهَا النَّاسُ قَدْ جَاءتْكُم مَّوْعِظَةٌ مِّن رَّبِّكُمْ وَشِفَاء لِّمَا فِي الصُّدُورِ وَهُدًى وَرَحْمَةٌ لِّلْمُؤْمِنِينَ

Yaa ayyuha an-naasu qad ja'atkum maw`izhatun min rabbikum wa shifaa'un limaa fi 's-sudoori wa hudan wa rahmatun li 'l-mu'mineen.

O Mankind! There has come to you a guidance from your Lord and a healing for (the diseases) in your hearts, and for those who believe a guidance and a mercy. *(Surah Yunus, 10:57)*

Allah ﷻ said "humanity," not only Muslims. "We sent realities and verses from Holy Qur'an," which might be from any verse of Holy Qur'an there is a secret, because He didn't say, "We send from some *aayaat* of Holy Qur'an," but rather, "*min al-qur'an*, from the entire Holy Qur'an," what is a cure for people, so that is in general. So for an expert—one whose heart and mind Allah opened and connected him to his guide, and from his guide to the Prophet ﷺ, and from Prophet ﷺ to Allah—that person will be able to understand the secrets of special *aayaat* and through reciting them will cure the sick.

From a Hadith of `Usama ibn Shareek ؓ as reported in the *Musnad* of Imam Ahmad, the Prophet ﷺ said:

عن ابن مسعود أن النبي صلى الله عليه وسلم قال: ما أنزل الله عز وجل داء إلا أنزل له دواء، علمه من علمه وجهله من جهله.

Allah did not send down any illness except He sent a cure with it and whoever knows it knows, and whoever was ignorant remained ignorant of it.

The point of this Hadith is *`alimahu man `alimahu*, "and whoever knows it knows." The secret of curing illnesses in the Holy Qur'an is not known to everyone, that is only known to a few people and those few can dive into meanings of Holy Qur'an and extract ways or verses to treat that person's specific sickness. For example, you tell a doctor that you have a headache, he gives you two tablets and the headache goes, but if you tell the doctor you have a headache and he gives a cream for your hand, that does not correspond to the sickness. So there are specific people who can dive into Holy Qur'an and find secrets in the specific verses to cure you and your family of illnesses. That is why the Prophet ﷺ said, "Only some know it and others do not."

The Hadith continues:

إن الله لم يضع داء إلا وضع له شفاء ، أو دواء ، إلا داء واحدا ، قالوا : يا رسول الله ما هو ؟ قال : الهرم

Treat the servants of Allah, for verily Allah does not put any illness except that He put its cure, except (regarding) one sickness. And they asked, "What is that?" and he ﷺ said, "al-haram, death. Other than that, Holy Qur'an can give cure to anyone."

This applies to both sicknesses of the soul and the body; the remedy for both is in Holy Qur'an, but there are conditions: you cannot do what you want and recite verses as you like and it will be done, as Allah ﷻ said:

فاسْأَلْ بِهِ خَبِيرًا

Fas'al bihi khabeera.

Ask (from) who is expert. *(Surat al-Furqaan, 25:59)*

You cannot ask just anyone as not everyone is an expert. You might ask someone and get an answer, but if he is not an expert his answer will not bring a change. Holy Qur'an needs one who is expert in Holy Qur'an, which means those whom Allah protected and called *'awliyaullah'*:

أَلا إِنَّ أَوْلِيَاء اللّهِ لاَ خَوْفٌ عَلَيْهِمْ وَلاَ هُمْ يَحْزَنُونَ الَّذِينَ آمَنُواْ وَكَانُواْ يَتَّقُونَ

Behold! Verily on the Friends of Allah there is no fear, nor shall they grieve; they who have attained faith and have always been conscious of Him.

(Surah Yunus, 10:62-63)

They fear not because they are given all this knowledge. Another Hadith narrated by Abu Dawood ﷺ:

عن جابر بن عبد الله قال : خرجنا في سفر فأصاب رجلا منا حجر ، فشجه في رأسه ، ثم احتلم ، فسأل أصحابه فقال : هل تجدون لي رخصة في التيمم ؟ قالوا : ما نجد لك رخصة ، وأنت تقدر على الماء ، فاغتسل ، فمات ، فلما قدمنا على رسول الله أخبر بذلك ، فقال : قتلوه قتلهم الله ألا سألوا إذا لم يعلموا ؟ فإنما شفاء العي السؤال إنما كان يكفيه أن يتيمم ويعصر - أو يعصب - على جرحه خرقة ثم يمسح عليها ، ويغسل سائر جسده .

We were traveling in a group and, by mistake, one of us was hit on the head and received a very severe wound. When that happened, that person immediately slept. Blood came out and we tried to fix it as much as we could. That young man slept and when he awoke he needed a ghusl (due to nocturnal emission). He asked his friends, "Do I have a rukhsa, permission to make tayammum (with dust or soil) and not with water?" We said, "No, you cannot, because the bleeding stopped so you cannot make tayammum, you must make ghusl (shower with water)." So the man took the shower, prayed, and afterwards he died. When we arrived to the Prophet ﷺ, we told him what happened and fa qaala an-Nabi ﷺ qataloohu, qaatalahumullah, Prophet ﷺ said we had killed him, and if we didn't know (what to do) why didn't we ask the one who knows? And `Ataa said, "It reached us that the Prophet ﷺ said, 'If he had washed his body and left out the head where the injury afflicted him [it would have sufficed].'"

So for every spiritual sickness there are spiritual tablets and for every physical sickness there are special verses from the Holy Qur'an to cure them. So you must ask the one who knows or otherwise you are killing the person by giving a recipe or prescription from yourself. If they didn't know why didn't they ask, for verily the cure for the sickness is one: to ask! You cannot try to cure yourself. Allah ﷻ cures you through His Holy Verses of Holy Qur'an and through Holy Hadith of the Prophet ﷺ. It was enough to make *tayammum*, as the Prophet ﷺ answered, instead of telling him to take a shower, which allowed water to enter his wound and caused an inflammation in his head, which killed him.

They made *fatwa* without knowledge. What is happening today? They make *fatwa* without knowledge and cause chaos everywhere, which is a sickness by itself! The Prophet ﷺ said he was able to make *tayammum,* to tie his wound with his hand and when it healed he could then use water in *wudu.* He could have wrapped his wound, place his wet hand on the bandage, that would have been enough for him to pray!

Prophet ﷺ said:

فأخبر أن الجهل داء ، وأن شفاءه السؤال

Ignorance is sickness and the cure is to ask.

So all of us are ignorant and to come out of ignorance is to ask. Allah ﷻ said in Holy Qur'an:

اسْأَلُوا أَهْلَ الذِّكْرِ إِن كُنتُمْ لاَ تَعْلَمُونَ

Ask the People of Dhikr (Holy Qur'an) if you don't know.

(Surat an-Nahl, 16:43)

So it is always important to ask the right people in order to get the right cure. All of us have sicknesses. We have physical illnesses and go to someone who knows and he gives us an answer, and sometimes we have spiritual sickness that we need to go to someone else for the cure. Allah ﷻ said that Holy Qur'an contains cure a for human beings, and:

وَنُنَزِّلُ مِنَ الْقُرْآنِ مَا هُوَ شِفَاء وَرَحْمَةٌ لِّلْمُؤْمِنِينَ وَلاَ يَزِيدُ الظَّالِمِينَ إَلاَّ خَسَارًا

And We sent down in the Qur'an such things that have healing and mercy for the believers. *(Surat al-'Israa, 17:82)*

So don't look right and left (for the cure), but go to those who know. And this Hadith is mentioned by Ibn Qayyim al-Jawziyya, a student of Ibn Taymiyya, in his book *Madarij as-Salikeen*, from Abi Sa`eed: *intalaqoo ba`d ashaab an-Nabi ﷺ fee safarin*, "A group of Companions ؓ of the Prophet ﷺ were travelling." You know in that time it was desert, and they travelled and reached an area where there was water and a date tree, and a small village among the palms. They asked the Arabs (Bedouins) to host them but they refused, which is not the custom of Arabs, and while discussing this the leader of the village was bitten by a scorpion or snake, we don't know exactly as they didn't say. His people tried every possible way to save their leader. You know the desert scorpion has a poisonous sting and can kill the person immediately. So they tried everything and couldn't cure him. Then they said, "Let us ask these people who just came; maybe they have knowledge or something with them that can cure him."

They approached those people and asked, "O people! Our leader has been bitten. We have tried everything and nothing is working!" So where did they go? They went to a guide, which means you need a guide. When you have a sickness or problem or you have to do business, or you have a question you must go to the one who knows something, not to a charlatan, who is flashy and just showing off, and who will deviate you! No, we are *Ahlu 's-Sunnah wa 'l-Jama`ah* and we follow the Prophet ﷺ, the Sahaabah ؓ and the Four Imams, and we don't accept anyone who deviates from *Siraat ul-Mustaqeem*! You must get a cure from someone who follows Shari`ah.

And they came to that group of Sahaabah ؓ and asked if they have anything to cure their leader. One of them said, *"W 'Allahi sa urqii,"* which is *ruqya*, to recite verses of the Holy Qur'an, which some Arabs call *'hijab,'* a veil to protect and save you, and some call *'taweez,'* which is from Holy Qur'an and it means to seek refuge in Allah from Shaytan. This is proof from Hadith of the Prophet ﷺ for those who say to not believe in them. He said, "W' Allahi, I can recite on the man to cure him but I will not, as you refused to host us. I am not going to recite for you until you give me compensation. If you had hosted us, we would do it and not take anything. Now we will do it, but you have to compensate us."

So the people discussed what they had to give the Sahaabah ؓ, who said, "You have to give one *qati`a min al-ghanam*, a herd of sheep," which may have been twenty, thirty or fifty sheep, Allah knows how many there were.

They said, "Okay, no problem, we will do it." Then, one Sahaabi ؓ recited *Surat al-Fatihah*, "Bismillahi 'r-Rahmani 'r-Raheem. Alhamdullahi Rabbi 'l-`Alameen. Ar-Rahmani 'r-Raheem. Maaliki yawm ad-deen. Iyyaka n`abudu wa iyyaka nasta`een. Ihdinas Siraat al-Mustaqeem. Sirat al-ladheena an`amta `alayhim ghayri 'l-maghdoobi `alayhim wa laa dhaalleen. Ameen," and spat (not blew) on the wound where the leader had been bitten. It was as if that leader had been tied with a chain that was suddenly taken away, and he was able to stand up and walk completely with no pain!

So the village people gave the Sahaabah ؓ the herd of sheep. Some Sahaabah ؓ said, "Let us divide the herd among us," while others said, "No, let us go to the Prophet ﷺ and whatever he decides, we will do."

So they took that herd of sheep to the Prophet ﷺ and mentioned what had happened to them.

He asked them, "How did you know that was *ruqya*? What you did is correct and put a share for me from what you got from them."

We know it is correct because they spit and recited *Surat al-Fatihah* on that sickness and Allah cured it.

There is so much explanation here! It means there are *ruqyas* that you recite and Allah ﷻ will accept, but we will come to that later, not now. The one reciting must be qualified and the one receiving must believe the recitation will benefit him, so both sides must have faith. The one reciting has to know that Allah ﷻ will cure, but he is doing what Allah said in Holy Qur'an, "We revealed what is healing to Mankind and a cure," and the one on the other side must know those are verses from Holy Qur'an that will cure him.

Therefore, sometimes you see the person is cured and sometimes you do not and that is based on belief. What the Sahaabi ؓ recited and spit on the wound corresponded to that particular sickness. It might be you are bit by a scorpion and read *Surat al-Fatihah* and you are cured, because the medicine for the bite of that creature was *Surat al-Fatihah*. However, everything he (the shaykh) recites has different affects and there are different ways to cure different sicknesses, but that is why the Prophet ﷺ said *Surat al-Fatihah* is for whatever it is read on. Also, that depends on the one reading: are they pure and clean, are they a guide, when they breathe can angels take their breath to the Divine Presence (i.e., is it pure)? So the success of that depends on many different elements and principles.

We leave it here and will continue in the evening. It is important for people to learn and understand. This is the beginning of the series on different illnesses and their cures as known in Islamic spirituality.

May Allah ﷻ forgive us and may Allah ﷻ bless us.

Wa min Allahi 't-tawfiq, bi ḥurmati 'l-ḥabīb, bi ḥurmati 'l-Fātiḥah.
And with Allah is success. For the sake of the Beloved, for his sake we recite the opening chapter of Holy Qur'an.

Allah Wants Us to be Persistent in Our Du`a

A'ūdhu billāhi min ash-Shayṭāni 'r-rajīm. Bismillāhi' r-Raḥmāni 'r-Raḥīm.
Nawaytu 'l-arbā'īn, nawaytu 'l-'itikāf, nawaytu'l-khalwah, nawaytu 'l-'uzlah,
nawaytu 'r-riyāḍa, nawaytu 's-sulūk, lillāhi Ta'alā fi hādhā 'l-masjid.
Atī'ūllāha wa atī'ū 'r-Rasūla wa ūlī 'l-amri minkum.
Obey Allah, obey the Prophet, and obey those in authority among you. (4:59)

Dastūr, madad yā Sulṭān al-Awlīyā, Mawlana Shaykh Nazim al-Haqqani ق.
Dastūr, madad yā Sulṭān al-Awlīyā, Mawlana Shaykh 'AbdAllah ad-Daghestani ق.

This is a continuation of this morning's lecture, so if you didn't attend you might not understand and I can't repeat what was said before, but I can summarize it in two sentences:

وَنُنَزِّلُ مِنَ الْقُرْآنِ مَا هُوَ شِفَاء وَرَحْمَةٌ لِّلْمُؤْمِنِينَ

Wa nunazzilu mina al-qur'ani ma huwa shifaa'un wa rahmatun li 'l-mu'mineen.

And We sent down in the Qur'an such things that have healing and mercy for the believers. *(Surat al-'Israa, 17:82)*

This a general statement for human beings and we explained this morning that whoever will recite certain verses will for sure be cured of illness, and they also use something called *ruqya, taweez* or *azimah,* whatever you call it, something that you hang.

In summary from the Hadith of the Prophet ﷺ, a group of Sahaabah ؓ traveled to a village and they were tired. They sought the leader of the village to host them, but he refused. They left, then suddenly the leader was bit by (something poisonous), a centipede, scorpion, tarantula or snake, so he was poisoned and fainted. Village residents tried to cure the leader and could not, so they came to the Sahaabah ؓ and said, "Do you have anyone who has power or knows how to treat someone bitten by a poisonous animal?"

One of them said, "Yes, we can."

The villagers said, "Then come with us."

The Sahaabah ﷺ said, "No, because you did not host us so you must give us compensation."

The village residents agreed to give a herd of sheep in compensation; they don't say here how many, but maybe it was 20-25 sheep. So that man came and began to recite *Surat al-Fatihah, "Alhamdullahi Rabbi 'l-`Alameen. ar-Rahman ar-Raheem. Maaliki Yawm ad-Deen...* (to the end). *Ameen.*" When he finished he spat on the leaders' wound, about which we know the Prophet ﷺ said in a Hadith:

ريق المؤمن شفاء

Reeq al-mu'min shifaa'.

The saliva of a believer is a cure.

Today when you say the word 'saliva' everyone recoils, but the Prophet ﷺ said, "The saliva of a *mu'min*, a believer," not only Muslim, but one who reached the level of sainthood. It means when you eat from what he gives you or eat from his leftovers or drink from his cup, it is *shifaa'*. In the time of the Prophet ﷺ there weren't a hundred cups, there was only one cup and all shared it. Today people drink from their own cup and don't share, although the Prophet ﷺ said the saliva of a believer is a cure.

That one was a Sahaabi ﷺ, so his saliva is pure and a cure as it had no sins. As soon as saliva entered the village leader's mouth, he was cured and stood up as if nothing had happened to him! So on their way back home they were discussing how to divide the herd they received and could not come to an agreement, so they left the matter to the Prophet ﷺ. And this is a very important matter about *ruqya*: in Islam, *ruqya* is accepted and not what they say today, that it is *bid`a* or *shirk*. (When they arrived home and the group of Sahaabah ﷺ reported this to Prophet), he ﷺ showed his acceptance of using *ruqya* in Islam by telling them, "Is there a share (of what you were compensated) for me?"

The compiler of this book was staying in Mecca and got sick. We explained in the last session who can recite *ruqya*; not everyone can do that because not everyone has clean breath going out and coming in. The breath coming in must be with *"Laa ilaaha illa-Llah"* and must go out with *"Laa ilaaha illa-Llah."* That breath must not ever backbite anyone or speak a false rumor or have sinned, so that Allah will accept his *ruqya.*

That author is a big `*alim* and he was in Mecca and got very sick. He could not find any doctor, *tabeeb*, someone who heals by Allah's Power. So he said, "I began to heal myself by myself, and what was the healing of myself by myself? It was reciting *Surat al-Fatihah* on my sickness, *wa laa ajid tabeeban wa laa dawa'an fa kuntu udawiyy nafsee bi qira'at al-fatihah*, as the Prophet ﷺ said, *al-fatihah lima quriyyat lah*, "*Surat al-Fatihah* is whatever you read it for," (i.e.) sickness, problems, an opening, and anything you want to do, Allah will accept and it will become easy.

And reading *Surat al-Fatihah* for *shifaa'* is very highly recommended by Prophet ﷺ. And he began to see a change, *ta'theera `ajeeba*, and said, "I feel myself being healed from reading *Surat al-Fatihah*. I used to have intense pain." We know today that intense pain may be cancer, who knows? He began to recite *Surat al-Fatihah* and saw something astonishing: the pain disappeared! He continues, "Whoever was sick in Mecca when I was there, I was curing them by reciting *Surat al-Fatihah*."

So there are certain cures for certain diseases and you cannot make a soup. Allah ﷻ gave *awliyaullah*, shuyukh or scholars from Prophetic Medicine, in which different verses of Holy Qur'an are recited to cure different illnesses. The verse that remedies depends on the sickness, and they will teach you and it will purify you and you will be able to cure your disease.

So the author of the book is testifying, and I chose it because it will be witness for those who are going to deny it and say this is *shirk*, those who follow the Salafi school of thought. This man who wrote the book, Ibn Qayyim al-Jawziyya, is a big scholar and a student of Ibn Taymiyya, and he is accepting (the validity of using) *ruqya*. Today they don't accept *ruqya*, they say it is *shirk*, but Ibn Qayyim al-Jawziyya mentioned it in his book in the Hadith of the animal that bit this man and agreed on the verses of Holy Qur'an that not everyone can do that state because it is specialized to those whose hearts Allah has opened to it, the *awliyaullah*, who differ from normal *mu'mins* or normal Muslims.

They say that everyone is a *wali*, and (we say) the *wali* is the one who is specialized and can give the *ayah* to be used for cure, and not only that: he emphasized that we have to be very careful on this matter, *hiya allatee tushfaa bihaa wa yulqaa bihaa*. He first mentioned "*adhkaar*" and then "*aayaat*;" he differentiated between recitation of *dhikrullah* and verses of Holy Qur'an," so that means he accepted there are people who can use *dhikrullah*, mentioning Allah's Beautiful Names and Attributes, in a way that can heal people from their sicknesses. And we know Allah's Ninety-nine Beautiful Names and Attributes, and He has Names that others don't know, which *awliyaullah* can use to heal and use Holy Qur'an to heal.

And he mentioned also that the *wali* can make *du`a* to heal and so through these three methods: *dhikrullah, ruqya/aayaat* and *du`a* as they can have full benefit and will heal completely.

We have mentioned that there are two kinds of illness, physical and spiritual, and the physical is easier than the spiritual. The physical can be cured and you are healed, but with spiritual illness you might die and still not be cured. What are these spiritual illnesses? They are illnesses of the self, seventeen different illnesses which include anger, hatred, malice and others that we have mentioned in the book *The Sufi Science of Self-Realization.*

And it is mentioned in `Abdullah ibn Ahmad ibn Hanbal's ﵁ book, *Al-Zuhd*, that in the time of the Bani Israel they were afflicted (with an illness) and they ran out into the desert as it was too much for them and they went out of the villages. Then Allah revealed to their prophet and said to them, "You are moving out of the village to the desert and still your bodies are dirty so you are carrying the dirtiness with you, and you are raising your hands to Allah, asking Him to take that illness away from you although your hands are full of the blood of people and your homes are full from forbidden wealth. Now when His Anger is so strong on you, you ask Him for forgiveness? You are not going to get it!"

And that means you must not try to heal someone if you know you are a sinful person, not clean; you must go to a clean person and ask them to make *du`a*. Do you think yourself to be a clean person or not? Can any of us raise our hands asking Allah or Prophet ﷺ (for our *du`as*) and say we are clean? None of us can, so how then are you going to be cured of your sickness? Look at Allah's Mercy! Despite all that, Allah still sends a cure.

What do we do when we get sick? We say, "O Allah! Take away that sickness and cure me." We do that in any religion. You are a chaplain (a *mureed*), don't they do that? So when in a problem, everyone seeks Allah's forgiveness and cure, so our focus is how to cure our bodies and get *shifaa'* and it is said that is the best way to cure yourself if you want to go on the route of not going to doctors.

There are medical doctors today who will treat you. If you want to go the route of using Holy Qur'an and the Holy Hadith of the Prophet ﷺ, for sure you will be cured, and that is through *du`a* that the Prophet ﷺ has taught his Sahaabah ؓ and through *du`a* from Holy Qur'an, as Allah ﷻ said:

وَقَالَ رَبُّكُمُ ادْعُونِي أَسْتَجِبْ لَكُمْ

Wa qaala rabbukumu 'd`oonee astajib lakum.
But Your Lord said, "Call on Me, I will answer you."   (al-Ghaafir, 40:60)

"Whatever you ask I will accept, but ask (Me)!" And when you ask and didn't get, don't say, "I didn't get," because you have to keep asking; Allah is testing you. Prophet ﷺ said, "For every sickness there is a cure except one, which is death."

What is the enemy of *du`a*? Why do you make *du`a*? Because you want to take away the affliction. So affliction is the enemy of the *du`a*, it is trying to stop the *du`a*. So that is why the Prophet ﷺ said from Sayyidina `Ali ؓ as mentioned by al-Hakim in his *Sahih*:

الدعا سلاح المومن

Ad-du`a silaah al-mu'min.
Du`a is the sword/weapon of the believer.

Three Levels of Du`a for Three Levels of Affliction

There are three different levels of *du`a* that are facing three different levels of affliction. *Du`a* is the weapon of the believer, the way you kill the enemy:

1) *Ad-du`a silaah al-mu'min*, the *du`a* is the weapon of the believer.
2) *Ad-du`a `imad ad-deen*, like *salaat*, *du`a* is the pillar of religion.
3) *Ad-du`a nooru 's-samawaati wa 'l-`ard*, and it is the Light of Heavens and Earth, as mentioned by Prophet ﷺ.

So *du`a* can take away everything and it can give you Noor of Heavens and Earth! It can be used as a weapon against Shaytan for what he does against your soul, and it will remove the bad desires and be a weapon against your sickness and a pillar for your religion!

Al-balaa'u thalaatha maqaamaat, he mentioned three levels of *du`a* that are facing three different levels of affliction:

1) One is the *du`a* that is stronger than the affliction and it will remove the affliction. That is why you need a guide, a shaykh that gives you strong *du`a* that will throw the affliction away.
2) The *du`a* that you didn't seek advice of a shaykh or *wali* to tell you which *du`a* you have to use against the *balaa* doesn't have power to take away the affliction, and therefore, the affliction will get stronger and take over.
3) The *du`a* and the affliction are equal in power and there will be a struggle. As long as you continue with your *du`a*, the affliction will be struggling and not cause you to fall down and as you increase in *du`a* that affliction will begin to decrease and disappear.

`Abdullah ibn `Sayyidina `Umar ﷺ narrated that the Prophet ﷺ said:

عن ابن عمر رضي الله عنهما قال : قال رسول الله صلى الله عليه وآله وسلم : " الدعاء ينفع مما نزل ، ومما لم ينزل ، فعليكم عباد الله بالدعاء "

Al-du`a yanfa` limaa nazal wa mimmaa nazal, fa `alaykum bi 'd-du`a.

The du`a will prevent the affliction from wherever already came down and also the affliction that might come later.* *(Al-Mustadrak `alaa as-Sahihayn)

We will continue this *inshaa-Allah* and mention the best *du`as* and the time for these invocations. And Allah ﷻ mentioned in Holy Qur'an:

يَمْحُو اللَّهُ مَا يَشَاءُ وَيُثْبِتُ وَعِندَهُ أُمُّ الْكِتَابِ

Yamhullaahu ma yashaa'u wa yuthbit wa `indahu umm al-kitaab.

Allah will erase or confirm whatever He likes and with Him is the Mother of Books. *(Surat ar-Ra`d, 13:39)*

Allah erases and confirms whatever He wants and the only thing that can erase what is written for you is the *du`a*. If, for example, it is written that you will go out of this door and fall and break your leg, that *du`a* will prevent it. So if you are aware of this and you begin everything you do with *du`a*—when you stand for prayer, upon entering a mosque, upon leaving your house, or when you wake up or sleep, or begin to speak with someone, etc.—and you begin by reciting *"Bismillahi 'r-Rahmani 'r-Raheem"* or *al-Fatihah* or *du`a*, then with the *barakah* of the *du`a* Allah will erase the *balaa*, difficulty, that was written for you that you are not seeing. May Allah open our eyes and our minds so we will always be on the right way!

And it is mentioned in a Hadith from Abu Hurayrah ؓ that the Prophet ﷺ said:

قَالَ أَبُو هُرَيْرَةَ : قَالَ رَسُولُ اللَّهِ صَلَّى اللَّهُ عَلَيْهِ وَسَلَّمَ : " مَنْ لَا يَسْأَلِ اللَّهَ يَغْضَبْ عَلَيْهِ

Who does not ask Allah, Allah will be angry with.

(Bukhari's Adab al-Mufrad, Musnad Ahmad and Ibn Majah)

Sometimes something happens to you and you begin to curse; no one thinks to make *du`a* instead of cursing. What is the benefit of cursing? I hear this from people or on TV, when people get something they don't like what do they say? They say something that begins with 's'. What is the benefit? That is on the tongue of everyone. I am sorry to say that this is someone who doesn't have *adab* in front of Allah or when he faces a problem he says "shit" instead of saying, *yaa Rabbee `afwak wa ridaak*, "O Allah, forgive me!" What is the benefit of bad words? It's not going to benefit them, but Shaytan puts them on the tongues of people and the first complaint they use against Allah is coming as the word "shit"! So we have to be very careful.

In that Hadith, Allah said, "Whoever doesn't ask from Him, Allah will get angry (*ghadab* Allah) with him." And you know "*ghadab* Allah" is very strong and the Prophet ﷺ said, "Be careful from your father's anger, as it will immediately affect your life." If your father says, "May Allah be angry with you!" that is a very heavy warning from the Prophet ﷺ to the children, so make sure you don't get that word out from your father's mouth! The mother is still softer (she will never be that angry), but the anger of the father is not accepted.

If that is for the anger of the father, so then what about the anger of the father's Creator? That is why whoever does not ask Allah, Allah will be angry with him. So when you face difficulty, why don't you say, *"alhamdulillah"* and *"shukran lillah,"* as that will immediately open forgiveness, and be thankful it was not worse instead of saying the 's' word! What do you need to say?

الخير فيما وقع

The best is in what happened.

Because it might have been a big accident in which you died, but instead Allah made it a smaller accident that involved paying some money to fix your car and saved you from injury or death! That is why we should always be asking Allah through *du`a* and that is the importance of *du`a*: it brings healing and takes affliction from you!

Sayyida `Ayesha ﵂ related that the Prophet ﷺ said:

إن الله يحب الملحين فى الدعاء

Truly Allah likes the one who keeps insisting (pestering) with the du`a.

Allah ﷻ will like that, so keep asking, "*Yaa Rabb, yaa Rabb* (help me)!" Allah likes that and keep bugging (pestering)! "Insisting" is not the right word; Prophet ﷺ said *al-mulihheen* is the one who overdoes it, so bug Paradise, bug the angels, saying, "*Allah, yaa Allah, yaa Allah, yaa Allah*!" then Allah will say, "*Yaa `Abdee*, O My servant!"

So Sayyida `Ayesha ﵂ said the Prophet ﷺ said that Allah likes the one who is always bugging, insisting, overdoing in asking Him. Therefore, O Muslims, O believers, O *mu'min*! Keep bugging, keep asking and keep praying and making *du`as* and you will be cured from many physical and spiritual sicknesses that you know or don't even perceive.

May Allah ﷻ forgive us and may Allah ﷻ bless us.

Wa min Allahi 't-tawfiq, bi ḥurmati 'l-ḥabīb, bi ḥurmati 'l-Fātiḥah.

And with Allah is success. For the sake of the Beloved, for his sake we recite the opening chapter of Holy Qur'an.

Allah Wants You to Persist in Asking Him

Aʿūdhu billāhi min ash-Shayṭāni 'r-rajīm. Bismillāhi' r-Raḥmāni 'r-Raḥīm.
Nawaytu 'l-arbāʿīn, nawaytu 'l-ʿitikāf, nawaytu'l-khalwah, nawaytu 'l-ʿuzlah,
nawaytu 'r-riyāḍa, nawaytu 's-sulūk, lillāhi Taʿalā fi hādhā 'l-masjid.
Atīʿūllāha wa atīʿū 'r-Rasūla wa ūlī 'l-amri minkum.
Obey Allah, obey the Prophet, and obey those in authority among you. (4:59)

Dastūr, madad yā Sulṭān al-Awlīyā, Mawlana Shaykh Nazim al-Haqqani ق.
Dastūr, madad yā Sulṭān al-Awlīyā, Mawlana Shaykh ʿAbdAllah ad-Daghestani ق.

In continuation of the other two *suhbahs,* we will further discuss the topic of divine healing. Any kind of *dhikrullah,* verses of Holy Qur'an or prayers, will heal us because they are Allah's Holy and Divine Words and every word carries unlimited miraculous power. The Holy Qur'an is not an ordinary book that people read and then put aside on the shelf. The Holy Qur'an is the Holy, Divine Words of Allah, His Uncreated Ancient Words, *Kalamullahi 'l-Qadeem.*

Today you go to so-called "healers" and they give you a different set of exercises to do and different forms of meditation that you can also perform in order to be healed, that is the goal. Sometimes that might work but not every time, because they are using their own blend of different ideas and different beliefs that they put together and they try to make you focus on that. Sometimes it works because there is an "influence."

As I mentioned before, a long time ago in Los Angeles I was in a conference on healing organized by Harvard University. They had conducted different experiments, and in one they placed a few sick people in a room and a healer from outside used different kinds of words, voices and sounds. The sick people in the room began to feel a change in their system. When the treatment ended after many such sessions, some people felt they had been healed, but there is always a question mark about such treatments. I am not going into a discussion about the conference, but it was very beneficial to present this form of healing in a scientific exposition.

One of the experiments they conducted was to use the recitation of the Holy Qur'an for healing. They placed a different machine all over the body to see if sickness responded to recitation of Holy Qur'an and they found organs began to respond and heal. Of course we know this for a fact, as they are Allah's Divine Words. I know one doctor from Florida who treats his patients only with the recitations of the Holy Qur'an. He places headsets on his patients, they listen to the recitations of the Holy Qur'an and get healed. So yes, it is possible to cure with what we explained yesterday, by *dhikrullah*.

As mentioned by Ibn Qayyim al-Jawziyya, who is from the school of Ibn Taymiyya, as long as Holy Qur'an is read by someone who is experienced and authorized, a patient can be healed by reciting *dhikrullah* and the verses of Qur'an and *du`as*. A person may be healed, but both sides must believe in the process: the patient has to believe that the holy verses are going to cure and the healer has to believe that *dhikrullah* is going to heal. If the healer does not have this belief and only heard from someone and tries to cure by reciting *dhikrullah*, it may or may not work because it depends on the one authorized to use it. That is why you see many people who use it without authorization might not cure their patients.

It is said the recitation is going to heal, as there is no doubt in *dhikrullah* and Holy Verses of Qur'an.

Sometimes doctors give medicine and it doesn't work on you or it might poison you as it has side effects. Also, if you give a strong dose of the verses of Holy Qur'an, because the verses carry a lot of energy and heavenly powers, so when it comes on someone who is not ready for it you may harm him or her, as Allah ﷻ said in Holy Qur'an:

لَوْ أَنزَلْنَا هَذَا الْقُرْآنَ عَلَى جَبَلٍ لَّرَأَيْتَهُ خَاشِعًا مُّتَصَدِّعًا مِّنْ خَشْيَةِ اللَّهِ وَتِلْكَ الْأَمْثَالُ
نَضْرِبُهَا لِلنَّاسِ لَعَلَّهُمْ يَتَفَكَّرُونَ

Law anzalnaa haadha 'l-quraana `alaa jabalin la-raaytahu khaashi`an mutasaddi`an min khashyatillaahi wa tilka 'l-amthaalu nadribuhaa li 'n-naasi la`allahum yatafakkaroon.

Had We sent down this Qur'an on a mountain, verily you would have seen it humble itself and cleave asunder for fear of Allah. Such are the similitudes that We propound to men that they may reflect. *(Surat al-Hashr, 59:21)*

"If We had sent down the Holy Qur'an on a mountain it would have shattered completely," because it cannot carry the manifestation of the Holy Qur'an. So when you give an *ayah* which has a strong influence on a patient who can take only a small dose you will destroy them with the big dose, and you cannot know the (proper) level. That is why in hospitals they say not to give an injection without a doctor's prescription, because they are responsible. Similarly, *awliyaullah* are responsible and are not given this knowledge to kill people, but to heal. So if you don't give the right dose you might not heal but kill; a bigger dose may kill and a lower dose might have no effect. Therefore, don't say the Holy Qur'an did not have an effect because it is your mistake, as you were unable to find the right dose to give from *dhikrullah* and verses of Holy Qur'an and *du`a*. That is why we say:

رب اشعث اغبر لو اقسم على الله لأبره

Rubba ash`ath aghbara law aqsama `ala allahi la-abbarah.

There may be a disheveled, dusty person who, if he swears an oath by Allah, Allah will fulfill it. *(Muslim)*

It means Allah ﷻ will not reject anyone through his outside appearance because He looks at the inside.

إن الله لا ينظر إلى اجسادكم ولا الى صوركم ولكن ينظر الى قلوبكم. رواه مسلم

Inna 'Llah laa yanzhuru ilaa ajsaadikum wa laa ila soowarikum wa laakin yanzhuru ila quloobikum.

Verily Allah does not look at your bodies nor at your appearances but He looks at your hearts. *(Muslim)*

Consistent Du`a is Better than Tricks of Charlatans

So for example, in some of the Sub-continent countries, you may go to a healer dressed in a Technicolor outfit like a rainbow, sitting on a couch with incense in front of him that he drops on fire to make smoke, then you suddenly hear him say, "ALLAH!" and everyone present becomes afraid and worried. Such people are charlatans. They cheat you by giving you herbal medicine that can make you drunk and is not a painkiller. They use an herb in Yemen similar to marijuana that makes you feel okay for a while, then you come back for more in a few days, but in reality you are poisoned. And although the place looks nice with big pictures all around, in reality you are being cheated. Instead, if you go to a poor and humble person sitting in a *masjid*, his recitation will cure you. This is because while he seems poor, his heart is not. That is why it depends from whom you are taking these *adhkaar* or who is reciting it for you. It is Allah Who cures and that one is advising you and cures by Allah's Divine Words.

So the first issue that we explained yesterday is *du`a*. Allah likes that His servant asks, and if you don't He is angry! Also, Allah is not happy with a servant who complains to someone other than Him. Today we go and complain everywhere and Allah does not like that, as He said:

وَقَالَ رَبُّكُمْ ٱدْعُونِى أَسْتَجِبْ لَكُمْ

Wa qaala rabbukum ad`oodnee astajib lakum.

And Your Lord says, "Call on Me, I will respond to you."

(Surah Ghaafir, 40:6)

But you have to keep asking as it is said in Islam:

Ajall al-karamaat dawaam at-tawfeeq.

The best of miracles is to be consistent.

This means constancy in your daily *dhikr*, so don't say, "I see no benefit," as it will come. You think doctors can give you benefit when they like? Allah gave them knowledge of different cures for physical medicine. He gave *awliyaullah* different divine verses from the Holy Qur'an not only to cure the physical body, but your soul as well. The importance is to the soul, as it returns to Allah and the body goes back to the earth. Look at how sick our soul is. That is why you must connect yourself to a guide who will guide you to different *awraad* in order to cure your different spiritual illnesses!

That is why we must *al-ilhaa fi 'd-du`a,* be persistent in asking. For example, if you go to a person and knock on their door saying, "I need a favor from you," they open the door and then close it. You come back another time and knock. They close the door again. Then you come back and keep coming back, until finally they open the door and say, "What do you want?"

You say, "Please, I need this favor from you."

Finally they say, "Alright, come in."

Allah likes His servant to keep bugging, so keep bugging and knocking (at His Door) and don't stop! Allah is never unhappy with someone who is begging and asking. That is why Sayyidina Abayazid ق was knocking and bugging consistently, although Allah ﷻ left him (without a reply) for many years. Does Allah not know His servant is knocking? He wants to see how much you keep bugging, because some people ask once or twice and then they stop. Allah does not like you to stop because He is the Creator and we are the servants, we are dependent on Him, so ask! And so Abayazid ق kept knocking and bugging, asking, "I'm here, I'm not going until You open Your door!" Allah sent an angel to ask him, "You want to come to Me?"

Kayf al-wusool ilayk? "How do I approach You?" as he didn't even know how to come to the Divine Presence. And because he was persistently bugging, Allah opened to Him sent him an angel telling him, *Utruk nafsaka wa ta`al,* "Leave your ego and come! If you want Me, that (ego) is your enemy."

You cannot have two in your heart, your heart has to carry One. Can a heart carry two people? It will fail. Allah gave every person one heart and that heart is inhabited by Allah ﷻ, Prophet ﷺ said:

قلب المو ءمن بيت الرب

Qalbu 'l-mumin baytu 'r-rabb.

The heart of the believer is the House of Allah.

And He said:

ما وسعني أرضي ولا سمائي ولكن وسعني قلب عبدي المؤمن

Maa wasi`anee ardee wa laa samaa'ee wa laakin wasi`anee qalbi `abdee al-mu'min.

Neither My Heavens nor My Earth contain Me, but the heart of My believing servant contains Me. *(Hadith Qudsee, Al-Ihya of al-Ghazali)*

So if you want to come, come! But keep asking, keep bugging, "I will open," that is al-*ilhaa* fi 'd-*du`a*.

It is related from Anas ؓ that the Prophet ﷺ said:

حَدِيثِ أَنَسٍ عَنِ النَّبِيِّ - صَلَّى اللَّهُ عَلَيْهِ وَسَلَّمَ : لَا تَعْجِزُوا فِي الدُّعَاءِ فَإِنَّهُ لَا يَهْلِكُ مَعَ الدُّعَاءِ أَحَدٌ .

Laa t`ajazoo fi 'd-du`a fa innahu laa yahlaku ma`a ad-du`ai ahad.

Don't be lazy with du`a, don't lose hope with du`a. No one will be destroyed with du`a. No one will lose when making du`a. (Haakim's Sahih)

"*Halak*" means destruction; no one who keeps on making *du`a* will be destroyed. *Du`a* keeps everyone safe. Too many people come and I will mention this story. Once someone brought a lady to see me in New York, she was carrying a child in her arms and she was crying. She is from Ivory Coast, his country.

He said, "She needs *du`a*." *Alhamdulillah*, with Mawlana's *barakah*, I have permission to do that or else it will be difficult on you if you have no permission.

I said, "What is your difficulty?"

She said, "They found a tumor in my head and it is not benign, it is cancer. They have given me two or three months to live."

What to do? As we are saying, make *du`a*. So I read *Surat al-Fatihah* on her head and on water seven times for her to drink and said, "May Allah make it easy, *Inshaa-Allah*."

She said, "I have an X-ray next week, an MRI." She went to take the X-ray and they called me by phone, saying the doctors checked the MRI and the tumor was gone! That is one case of many.

The week before last, there was one lady who comes from New Jersey and she has a daughter-in-law who for many years was not becoming pregnant. Every time I go there she says they have no children. So I said, "Be patient and keep making *du`a*." This time she came and said, "My daughter-in-law is pregnant!" How many hundreds and thousands came to Mawlana ق and Grandshaykh ق and were cured? The cure is not because of yourself, but because you are connected to *awliyaullah* who gave permission on their behalf; the cure was not even coming from them, but they are a means to take that petition to Prophet ﷺ and he takes it to Allah ﷻ, Who cures you as *Allahu ash-Shafee*! Guides take you to reach there and they teach you how to ask through *du`a*.

Sayyida `Ayesha ؓ said that Prophet ﷺ said:

قَالَ رَسُولُ اللَّهِ - صَلَّى اللَّهُ عَلَيْهِ وَسَلَّمَ : إِنَّ اللَّهَ يُحِبُّ الْمُلِحِّينَ فِي الدُّعَاءِ .

Inna 'Llah yuhibbu 'l-mulihheenu fi 'd-du`a.

*Allah loves those who are always persistent in du`a.* (al-Awza`ee)

It means asking non-stop. Don't say it didn't happen! It is happening, it is written and it will happen according to how much you persist! I don't want to give this example, it is a bad example, but there are many people who I see at grocery stores buying the lottery tickets and they have never won, but are persistent, thinking, "One day I will win." How do they have that determination for the lottery, which Allah forbade for Muslims, and you don't have such faith in Allah? You have to say to yourself, "Allah will respond to me," but you must persist, *ilhaa bi-du`a*, "to be persistent in *du`a*," that is the topic of this chapter.

He gave an example in *Kitaab az-Zuhd* by Imam Ahmad:

وَفِي كِتَابِ الزُّهْدِ لِلإِمَامِ أَحْمَدَ عَنْ قَتَادَةَ قَالَ : قَالَ مُوَرِّقٌ : مَا وَجَدْتُ لِلْمُؤْمِنِ مَثَلًا إِلَّا رَجُلٌ فِي الْبَحْرِ عَلَى خَشَبَةٍ ، فَهُوَ يَدْعُو : يَا رَبِّ يَا رَبِّ لَعَلَّ اللَّهَ عَزَّ وَجَلَّ أَنْ يُنْجِيَهُ .

`An-Qataada qaal, qaala mooriqun: maa wajadtu li'l-mu'mini mathalan illa rajulun fi'l-bahri `alaa khashabatin, fahuwa yada`u: yaa Rabb! ya Rabb! la`ala 'Llaha `azza wa jall yunjiyyahu.

Qataada said, "One person said, 'I found an answer, a way for mu'mins, an example of persistence. If someone is in the middle of an ocean and a storm came and broke the boat, what would he do to save himself? He would jump on one of these wooden boats/planks and then he would float. Is that enough? No, he would also say, 'Yaa Rabb!' How many times would he say it? He would keep saying, 'Yaa Rahman, yaa Allah, yaa Raheem!' and he would never stop until he reaches safety. But if you say it once and stop, you might not reach safety.'"

Allah likes someone who is persisting, *al-mulih fi 'd-du`a*, as when He asked, "What do you want, *yaa* Abayazid? You are knocking, knocking, what do you want?!"

"I want You."

"Okay, come to Me but leave your ego behind! You want Me? My Door is open." He said this at the end after He had given him a hard time, like He gave Sayyidina Ahmad Badawi a hard time.

He kept knocking on the door, "*Yaa Rabbee, yaa Rabbee, yaa Rabbee!*" and he heard a voice say, "What do you want?"

Before when he was knocking, one person came and said, "*Yaa* Ahmad! You need the key to enter the Divine Presence? I have the key for you."

He said, "No, no, I'm not taking the key from you!" this is arrogance, he was on that level of arrogance.

"From whom do want it then? I have the key for you, come and take it!"

"No, I want it from Allah, the Key-Maker!"

He said, "Okay."

Allah left him like that, and every moment he kept saying, "*Yaa Rabbee* open, *yaa Rabbee* open, *Yaa Rabbee* open!"

After six months Allah opened and he heard a voice saying, "*Yaa* Ahmad, you want the key?"

He said, "*Yaa Rabbee,* I want the key!"

Angels are saying to him, "Okay, the key is with that man (you turned away), go and find him."

Now he was at the mercy of that man. Allah had sent the key but he hadn't taken it. Don't let you arrogance play with your ego, it will change you easily! After six months that man showed up again and said, "You want the key?"

"Please!"

"Okay," look how long they kept him persisting to open, to get something. He said, "Now I want the price, before it was free."

He said, "How much?"

He said, "I don't want your money, all the money of *dunya* is not enough for the key. I need your knowledge. That knowledge you built on arrogance, we don't like it, we want to take it away from you." Today all scholars build on arrogance, but not *awliyaullah* they are not arrogant and that is why their *du`a* is accepted immediately that is why you need to go to a *wali* and ask him to make *du`a* for you. That's why we got to *awliyaullah;* look for them, where are they? There are 124,000 *awliya* in every time; one dies, one comes. There are not only the forty *wali*s at high level, but you cannot refuse the others, you cannot disrespect them, you have to respect them. Out of 124,000 there are only 7,007 Naqshbandi and the rest are from other *tariqahs*, so you have to respect everyone. Sayyidina Ahmad Badawi ق was from the Badawiyya Tariqah, not the Naqshbandi Tariqah, and this is his story. We don't respect it? There are 3-4 million who go to his *masjid/maqaam* every year in Egypt!

So he said, "Okay, look into my eyes," and Ahmad ق looked into his eyes and he took all his knowledge, he didn't even know how to recite *Fatihah,* and then he left him. But he was persisting even when the children used to run after him and throw stones at him, saying, "Shaykh al-Islam went crazy!" He was beaten up but he was persistent, so be persistent!

After another six months that *wali* came back and poured into Ahmad Badawi's ق heart all this heavenly knowledge, then no one in his time could look in his eyes and thereafter he always wore a *burqah* covering his eyes so no one could look or they fainted from the light in them (that he received) because he was persistent and for two years he never stopped asking. So we must not stop asking, keep asking and Allah will open!

This is *al-Ilhaa fi-Du`a.* Next time we will go into (the chapter) "*Al-Afaat Alatee Tamn`a Athara ad-Du`a,* The different kinds of affliction or bad things that prevent the acceptance of the *du`a* and prevent it from doing its job (being accepted)."

Be what? Be persistent in *du`a*! Don't say, "I didn't get an answer," never mind, because if you don't get an answer you are not losing when you make *du`a* to Allah ﷻ! He will grant you many rewards because He knows you are humble and you are asking.

May Allah forgive us, may Allah cure us, may Allah clean us, may Allah keep us with Prophet ﷺ, may Allah keep us with Mawlana Shaykh Nazim ق in *dunya* and *Akhirah,* with Grandshaykh ق, *yaa Rabbee, yaa Allah,* and give us from what He gave to Prophet ﷺ and dress us from the manifestation of His Prophet ﷺ and extend our life to see Mahdi عليه السلام and `Isa عليه السلام!

May Allah ﷻ forgive us and may Allah ﷻ bless us.

Wa min Allahi 't-tawfiq, bi ḥurmati 'l-ḥabīb, bi ḥurmati 'l-Fātiḥah.

And with Allah is success. For the sake of the Beloved, for his sake we recite the opening chapter of Holy Qur'an.

Conditions of Du`a and How to Perfect It

A'ūdhu billāhi min ash-Shayṭāni 'r-rajīm. Bismillāhi' r-Raḥmāni 'r-Raḥīm.
Nawaytu 'l-arbā'īn, nawaytu 'l-'itikāf, nawaytu'l-khalwah, nawaytu 'l-'uzlah,
nawaytu 'r-riyāḍa, nawaytu 's-sulūk, lillāhi Ta'alā fī hādhā 'l-masjid.
Atī'ūllāha wa atī'ū 'r-Rasūla wa ūlī 'l-amri minkum.
Obey Allah, obey the Prophet, and obey those in authority among you. (4:59)

Dastūr, madad yā Sulṭān al-Awlīyā, Mawlana Shaykh Nazim al-Haqqani ق.
Dastūr, madad yā Sulṭān al-Awlīyā, Mawlana Shaykh 'AbdAllah ad-Daghestani ق.

Allah is the Creator! Allah doesn't need anyone, everyone is in need of Him! In order to give the *ummah* the best of this *dunya* and *Akhirah,* He gave us Sayyidina Muhammad ﷺ, and the greatness of the Prophet ﷺ is from the Greatness of Allah ﷻ, and what the Prophet ﷺ showed us we follow, and for sure we are weak servants, helpless! Even if you become a leader you are still helpless. We are still struggling.

Grandshaykh `AbdAllah ق liked to tell this story that some people might say is not nice, but it has big wisdom in it. There was a king who invited to his presence many people and he fed them. One time one of the invitees had with him a *majdhoob,* someone in a trance who is always attracted in Allah's love and he says things that people don't understand, although for sure he understands and *awliyaullah* understand.

So he invited that *majdhoob* to come along and the king offered the food and was happy looking and eating with them, and the *majdhoob* said, "O my king! The best thing in life is to pee (urinate) and to go to restroom (defecate)!"

At this, the king was upset. He said, "Who brought you here?"

The *majdhoob* said, "This man brought me here."

So the king said, "Take him to prison, that one is *majdhoob*!" and he continued to say, "The best thing in life is to pee and go to the restroom!"

The king cursed him and the *majdhoob* ran away, but he made a *du`a* (and we have to be persistent in our *du`a*), "May Allah not make you pee and not go to the restroom!" and then he ran away like a bird and no one could catch him.

The next day the king could not go to the bathroom or do anything (to relieve himself) and the next day it was the same. He brought all doctors, homeopaths, etc., but no one could cure him, and finally he realized the only one who can cure him is that *majdhoob*, so he sent for him.

That *majdhoob* came strutting like a hero and asked him, "O King! Do you accept what I said?

The king said, "Yes."

He said, "Okay, then say it publicly!"

The king said, "The best thing in life is to go to the restroom and pee."

The *majdhoob* was teaching him that if Allah ﷻ pulls one favor out you will be imbalanced and "you need that *majdhoob* to balance you." Although the king brought all kinds of doctors to help him, they couldn't, which was to show him that everything is in balance. If you have a problem, you must try to solve that problem and to keep nice everything nice that Allah ﷻ gave you. If there is a problem ask Allah ﷻ.

Our belief is that everything is from Allah—what is good is from Him and what is bad is from us. So if someone comes and tells you, "I am seeing something wrong in you, try to fix it," who pushed that person to say that? Is it not Allah also? Since we surrender and submit (to Allah) we must submit to what everyone says, as it is Allah Who makes him or her speak, to bring your attention to a particular issue. If someone keeps quiet, that is okay, but if someone mentions something to you for your own good, follow that!

Don't be like Sayyidina Musa ؑ who said to Sayyidina Khidr ؑ, "I'll go along with you," but later refused to accept when Khidr ﷺ made a hole in the boat and he said, "Why are you making a hole in the boat? You're going to make everyone to fall in the ocean!" In fact, Khidr ؑ had done that in order to prevent a tyrant king from coming and seizing the boat but that [knowledge] was hidden from Sayyidina Musa ؑ. So there are certain things you must follow [without question].

Why is there Prophetic Medicine? Why did the Prophet ﷺ cure people when he could have left it and said, "Leave it as it is, there is nothing to be done." But this *dunya* is created with *asbaab*, causes: you do something, you get something. So whatever he gives you, you must follow.

As we mentioned in the prior session, a group of Sahaabah ؓ went to a village where the leader of that village was bitten by a poisonous scorpion.

The Sahaabah ﷺ cured him by reciting *ruqya* on him, which they were later compensated for. When they returned to the Prophet ﷺ, he asked them to give him a share of (their compensation), which means he was indicating, "I am approving that everyone needs someone specialized in the particular pain he or she is in."

It means there are some professionals who can check you. Why are people coming here? There is a spiritual cure for our souls in the words coming here that have been inherited through a spiritual chain from Mawlana Shaykh Nazim ق to Grandshaykh ق and all the way to the Prophet ﷺ. Whatever spiritual sickness the soul is inflicted by, there is a spiritual cure for them here. People come in order to be healed from their spiritual sickness. Why do we do *dhikr* every week? Although it is not an obligation, we do it every week. Grandshaykh `AbdAllah ق and Mawlana Shaykh Nazim ق insist on attending the weekly *dhikr* for two reasons. If you don't want to do it, don't do it, but for those who attend *dhikr* every week, Allah ﷻ will waive whatever sins they have done from one week to another. Is that good or bad? It is good, so should we do it or not? The second reason, everyone who attends *dhikrullah, kaffaaratan li saba`een majlis soow,* 70,000 evil associations around your area will be cleansed from the *barakah* of your *dhikr* gathering! Yet this is only through one person from the gathering; for two people it will be 70,000 multiplied by 2, for three people, 70,000 multiplied by 3, and so on. So we must know that illnesses, both spiritual or physical, can be cured in any different way.

How to Perfect Your Du`a

Be persistent in making *du`a*, don't stop.

As we said in the previous lectures, the Prophet ﷺ insisted that this (healing) has to be done through *du`a*: *al-ilhaah bid'-du`a,* continue on your position with determination. Allah ﷻ likes when you keep insisting and continue making *du`a*, as the Prophet ﷺ said:

مَنْ لَمْ يَسْأَلِ اللّه يَغْضِبْ عَلَيْهِ

Man lam yas'ali-Llaahi yaghdib `alayh.

Whosoever does not supplicate to Allah, He will be angry with Him.

(Tirmidhi)

So when you don't ask Allah ﷻ, He gets angry with you. Ask Him and keep asking! Be persistent in your *du`a*. Don't say, "I made *du`a* but it didn't work, so I will stop." No, don't stop! When people want to receive grants, they submit paperwork and if they don't get it they submit it again and again, until finally they say, "What is the benefit? We did our best, but it didn't work," and they stop. They also say, "Those people submitted their grant paperwork and got it (immediately); they received the grant, but we didn't!" You are not them, as they are *dunya* people and you are *Akhirah* people. If you didn't get it, continue to be persistent as Allah ﷻ likes that!

Ajalla al-karamaat dawaam at-tawfeeq.

The best of miracles is to be consistent (in what you are doing).

We pray five times a day. Can you say the next day, "I prayed yesterday so (I don't have to pray now)"? No, you have to pray! Some say, "Don't celebrate the Prophet's birthday," as they have their own ideas. But Sayyidina Abu Hamid al-Ghazali ق observed the birthday of Prophet ﷺ year after year, as that was how it was in that time. Although he was a big scholar, he had doubts (*mutashakkik*). It was Monday, 12 *Rabi` al-Awwal* and he was writing something important which, at that time, was necessary to get it out immediately. Suddenly, a black fly came and began to drink the ink from his pen, for which Imam Ghazali ق stopped moving his hand as he didn't want it to fly off. He said, "Allah ﷻ created me from *Ummat an-Nabi* ﷺ for the sake of the Prophet ﷺ just as He created this fly for the sake of the Prophet ﷺ, so I will keep it until it quenches its thirst." That night *inaayatullah* was coming down on the 12th *Rabi` al-Awwal*, as not every year it coincides on a Monday.

Similarly for Hajj, you ask your shaykh whether you should go for Hajj this year or not and if he doesn't give permission don't go, as *awliyaullah* can see if the Manifestation of Allah ﷻ will come on the hujjaj on `Arafat or not. If it is not, they tell you don't go, and otherwise, they tell you to go. So you need to keep asking each year until you get permission and go. Don't stop asking, saying, "I'm not going as Shaykh is not giving permission." Keep asking! How many times we asked your grandfather (Mawlana Shaykh Nazim) if we can we go for Hajj and he told us, "Go next year," and when the next year comes, he says, "Next year," and 'next year' comes, again he says, "Next year." Then he says to others, "You go," but for us he says, "Don't go." That is a test, but still you persist (in trying to go).

So the fly was quenching its thirst and Imam Ghazali ﷺ persisted in observing that night of 12th *Rabi` al-Awwal* that year when that *tajalli* came down and Allah ﷻ opened all his spiritual powers. Similarly with people who apply for grants, they keep asking and asking, perhaps they ask non-stop for fifteen years, but they never get it until it opens suddenly! You are not *dunya* people, you are *Akhirah* people, and Allah gives when he sees you are patient. So persist in your *du`a* as Allah is happy with His Servant when He sees His Servant is persistent and keeps asking and asking!

What Prevents Du`a from Being Accepted

Now we come to the issue of *al-aafaat allatee tamna` athara 'd-du`a*, the various elements or things that forbid/prevent the *du`a* from being accepted.

The servant slows down in his asking.

People know the importance of making *du`a*, but they don't know why their *du`a* is not accepted. Our obligation is to make *du`a* and it is not our duty to say that Allah accepted it or not. Just as you are obliged to pray *Salaat azh-Zhuhr* every day and cannot say, "I already prayed yesterday (so need to pray today)," your duty is to make *du`a*! The first thing that prevents *du`a* from being accepted is when the servant slows down or increases too much in asking: one day he asks too much and the next day he says, "I asked too much but Allah didn't accept, so I will not ask again. Whenever He wants to give, He will give." So he stops, and Allah ﷻ doesn't like that. *Fa yastahsir wa yada` ad-du`a,* he will drop the *du`a* and he will not continue. This is one of the elements that prevent your *du`a* from getting accepted. So your duty is to make *du`a* and it's not your business if it is accepted or not, as Allah knows best!

An example of this is when someone plants seeds in his garden and begins watering them, then finally he gets tired and stops watering and taking care of his garden. What will happen? All his plants will die, they will finish! When the stem was about to come out, he stopped and left it. This is an example of a person who constantly makes *du`as*, but right when his *du`a* is about to reach its peak and get accepted, he stops. Shaytan whispers in your ear, "Why do you want to make *du`a* today?" But when you stop, that *du`a* is dead; it will no longer be accepted because you let Shaytan throw his seeds into your heart, destroying that nice plantation planted by divine *du`as* that Prophet ﷺ used to make! Shaytan throws in them something with a bad smell and destroys that whole *du`a* you were making!

Do not rush your *du`a.*

It was mentioned by Imam Abu Hurayrah ؓ in *Sahih Bukhari* that the Prophet ﷺ said:

يُسْتَجَابُ لِأَحَدِكُمْ مَا لَمْ يُعَجِّلْ يَقُوْلُ دَعَوْتُ فَلَمْ يُسْتَجَابُ لِي

Yustajaabu li-ahadikum maa lam yu'ajjil yaqoolu da`awtu fa lam yustajaabu lee.

The du`a of any one of you will be answered so long as he is not impatient and says, 'I made du`a, but it was not answered.'"

Allah will accept your *du`a* if you are not trying to rush it! Keep reciting it every day with all your heart and don't rush like those who rush to make a deadline and you see them writing their paper in the last moment, rushing and rushing, and they make many mistakes in rushing. Prophet ﷺ said, "Don't rush your *du`a,* keep doing it."

Ajalla al-karamaat dawaam at-tawfeeq.

The best of miracles is the continuity of what you are doing.

When you rush you don't get anything! Allah will not give it to you, then you say, "I asked and my *du`a* was not accepted." That is why it is recommended that when you need a *du`a,* go to those whom you know are sincere servants of Allah as they have been given authorization from their guides, like the Sahaabah ؓ were given from Prophet ﷺ: like *aimmah* given from Sahaabah ؓ and like *awliyaullah* given from a'immah, so you go to them and they make *du`a* for you and you see that your *du`a* is completely accepted.

As narrated by Sayyidina Anas ؓ in *Musnad Ahmad,* the Prophet ﷺ said:

فِي مُسْنَدِ أَحْمَدَ مِنْ حَدِيثِ أَنَسٍ قَالَ : قَالَ رَسُولُ اللَّهِ - صَلَّى اللَّهُ عَلَيْهِ وَسَلَّمَ : لَا يَزَالُ الْعَبْدُ بِخَيْرٍ مَا لَمْ يَسْتَعْجِلْ ، قَالُوا : يَا رَسُولَ اللَّهِ كَيْفَ يَسْتَعْجِلُ ؟ قَالَ : يَقُولُ قَدْ دَعَوْتُ رَبِّي فَلَمْ يَسْتَجِبْ لِي .

Laa yazaal al-`abdu bi khayrin maa lam yasta`jil. Qaaloo ya Rasoolullahi kayfa yast`ajilu? Qaal: yaqoolu qad da`awtu rabbee falam yastajib lee.

The servant is always in a good way as long as he does not rush. They asked: O Prophet of Allah, how does he rush? He ﷺ said, "He says, 'I prayed to my Lord and He did not respond to me.'"

Allah ﷻ doesn't like people who rush their *du`a*, so keep making *du`a* but don't rush, as the Prophet ﷺ said:

وَفِي صَحِيح مُسْلِمٍ عَنْهُ : لَا يَزَالُ يُسْتَجَابُ لِلْعَبْدِ ، مَا لَمْ يَدْعُ بِإِثْمٍ أَوْ قَطِيعَةِ رَحِمٍ ، مَا لَمْ يَسْتَعْجِلْ ، قِيلَ : يَا رَسُولَ اللَّهِ مَا الِاسْتِعْجَالُ ؟ قَالَ يَقُولُ : قَدْ دَعَوْتُ ، وَقَدْ دَعَوْتُ ، فَلَمْ أَرَ يُسْتَجَابُ لِي ، فَيَسْتَحْسِرُ عِنْدَ ذَلِكَ وَيَدَعُ الدُّعَاءَ .

Laa yazaalu yustajaabu li'l-`abdi maa lam yadu` bi-ithmin aw qati`atee rahimin maa lam yasta`jal. faqeela: Yaa Rasoolullahi maa'l-isti`jaal? Qaala yaqoolu qad da`awtu wa qad da`awtu falam ara yastajaabu lee. Fa-yatahasir `inda dhalika wa yadau` ad-du`aa.

Allah rejects supplications if the worshipper is hasty or does not have patience. It was asked, "O Messenger of God! What does it mean to be hasty?" The Prophet ﷺ said, "A worshipper says, 'I have prayed and prayed, and I don't yet see that it will be accepted," so he gives up hope of being answered and leaves making du`a." (Muslim from Abu Hurayrah, Sahih al-Jami #7705)

So the Sahaabah ﵃ asked the Prophet ﷺ, "What does it mean to rush?" and he replied, "When he says, ';I asked Allah but He didn't respond!' " This means, he rushed for his *du`a* to be accepted. Don't rush! Whenever Allah wants, that is when He will accept your *du`a*.

Conditions for Du`a to be Accepted

Focus wholeheartedly on what you are asking and correct guidance will come.

What are the conditions for *du`a* to be accepted? When you are making *du`a*, focus on the specific issue you are making *du`a* for. For example, "I'm making *du`a* to get healthy!" as many people today remember to make *du`a* only when they are sick. So do *muraqabah* and focus your thoughts and your heart on your sickness. *Hudoor al-qalb wa jam`eeyatuhu bi kulliyatihi ma` al-matloob,* during your *du`a*, make sure you are focusing on the issue that is before you. For example, if someone tells you, "I want my daughter/son to get married," "I want my son to get good grades," or "My son is applying for college," try to focus well and bring your heart toward the *du`a* you need to recite in order for it to become a perfect medicine for that issue or sickness, and like giving medicine, you have to give the right one in order to treat the disease.

You have to go back to the previous three lectures in order to fully understand what we are saying. There are *du`as* the guide will guide you that are perfect in fixing your problem. Not every *du`a* is going to have the same effect for your problem, as each *du`a* differs from one person to another.

I will give an example, as I did previously with many other examples about cancer and conceiving a child, and so on. There is a lady in Texas whose name I will not mention, although I think many people here know her. Her daughter was trying to get into medical school for many years, and her test scores were always around 73 or 74 (not passing). Each time her mother came to me, I told her to let her daughter retake the test. I remember telling her to take it four times, which she did, and she kept getting 73 or 74—not enough to get accepted for residency. Finally, she came again last year and said, "My daughter is thinking of studying another specialty," and I told her, "There is no harm if she takes the test again." She retook the test and this time got an 80 (passed)!

It's not from me but from the *barakah* of our shaykh, Mawlana Shaykh Nazim al-Haqqani ق. After many years of struggling, she got accepted in Boston. We pushed her to not give up and Allah accepted. If we had rushed and given up after the first year, saying, "O! It didn't work out so you don't need to do that..." (the outcome would have changed). I was continuously pushing her to repeat and repeat, although she and her mother were fed up. She repeated it and got it! The *du`a* is what caused her to get that position and it's from Allah ﷻ, no one else.

Best Times to Make Du`a and Fulfilling what is Prescribed

There are times best for making *du`a* and if it coincides in one of these times, for sure your *du`a* will be accepted, and Allah ﷻ accepts all *du`as*, as He said:

ادْعُونِي أَسْتَجِبْ لَكُمْ

Id`oonee astajib lakum.

Supplicate to Me and I will give you! *(Surat al-Mu'min, 40:60)*

But ask! If you don't get in *dunya* you might get it in the grave, where Allah will give you better than what you were asking. There are six times in which *du`a* is most accepted:

1. ***Ath-thuluth al-akheer min al-layl.* The last third of the night before *Salaat al-Fajr* by two hours**, which is the time of qiyam when everyone is sleeping. At that time you can focus well and meditate on what you are asking and the *du`a* you got from your guide. Sit at that time and do it, but don't say, "I did it" like some people, when we give them something to recite for forty days and they call us on the 39th day, saying "Should I continue or stop?" What is the issue if you continue? Continue! Why do you want to stop? Do it one time, two times, three times, four times, continue! Therefore, when you want to make a *du`a* in the last third of the night, do it continuously unless you are traveling, sick or with a guest.

2. ***Ba`d al-adhaan.* When the *adhaan* is being called** [*adhaan* sounds], like right now. May Allah ﷻ give us long life to see Mahdi ؑ and give *shifaa`* to us and to Mawlana Shaykh Nazim ق! May He make everyone happy with their family, for those who just got married to be happy with their wives and those who are not married to get married and for everyone to be happy with their children, both in *dunya* and in *Akhirah*, and to be with Prophet ﷺ! *Fatihah*. (We said) "*adhaan*" and the *adhaan* came! But we don't stop and say, "O! Since we did it on the right time, this is a *karamah*." No, there is a wisdom here to show us that Allah ﷻ wanted us to make a *du`a* at that exact moment when the *adhaan* was being called when we mentioned it, to show that perhaps there is a benefit in it.

3. ***Bayn al-adhaan wal-iqaamah.* Between the *adhaan* and *iqaamah*,** the time when you wait about five minutes after the calling of *adhaan* just before the *iqaamah*.

4. ***Adbaar as-salaat al-maktubaat.* After the *fard* prayers**. Any *du`a* you make at that time is also accepted.

5. ***Wa `inda su`oodil imaam yawmi 'l-jum`ah `ala 'l-mimbar hatta taqdi as-salaat min dhaalika 'l-yawm.* On Friday when the imam goes up on the *minbar* to give his *khutbah***. Make *du`a* through your heart, but not by holding beads in your hand since *khutbah* is considered to be part of prayer and holding beads is not accepted at that time. So make *du`a* through your heart and think about it until the *khutbah* and the prayer is finished.

6. ***Wa aakhiru sa`atin ba`ad al-`asr.* The last hour after *Salaat al-`Asr*,** one hour before *Maghrib*.

Finally, the one thing all of these times have in common is *khushu`*, sincerity in the heart, which means to focus well on your *du`a* despite the whispers. The best *du`a* in these six times is the *du`a* made from a broken heart, in a state of helplessness and weakness, in-between the Hands of Allah, as you are at His Door. In order for your *du`a* to be accepted, turn toward your Lord in humility, face the *qiblah*, and ask Him!

We have mentioned six different places (occasions) when *du`a* can be done and it is accepted, which doesn't mean *du`a* cannot be done anywhere else and cannot be accepted; no, it can be accepted, but this is more acceptable and more quick to be accepted than in the other times. And we mentioned these six different places that I think everyone has (written); if anyone doesn't have them they can go back to Sufilive.com and check them, *Inshaa-Allah*. Let's go through them quickly.

Best Times to Make Du`a

1) الثلث الاخير من ال يل The last third of the night.

2) وعند الأذان When the *adhaan* is being called.

3) الأذان والاقامة بين Between the *adhaan* and *iqaamah.*

4) ادبار الصلوات المكتوبات After the *fard* prayers.

5) وعند صعود الامام يوم الجمعة على المنبرحتى تقضى الصلوة On Friday when the imam goes up on the *minbar* to give his *khutbah,* until the prayer is finished.

6) وآخر ساعة بعد العصر The last hour before *Maghrib* on *Jumu`ah* day.

Conditions of Making Du`a

1) وكان على طهارة To have full *wudu.*

2) واستقبل الداعي القبلة To sit facing *qiblah.*

3) بدأ بحمد الله والثناء عليه To praise Allah and thank Him.

4) ثم ثنى بالصلوة على محمد عبده صلى الله عليه وسلم To make *salawaat* on the Prophet ﷺ.

5) The *du`a* has an opening; you do not enter a house without knocking, it is *adab* to knock at the door.

Begin the Du`a

To enter in the Divine Presence of Allah ﷻ so that the Door will be opened, you must first read:

بِسْمِ اللّهِ الرَّحْمَنِ الرَّحِيمِ الحَمْدُ للهِ رَبِّ العَالَمِينَ والصلاة والسلام على اشرف
المرسلين سيدنا محمد و على اله و صحبه اجمعين

Bismillahi 'r-Rahmani 'r-Raheem alhamdulillahi rabbi 'l-`alameen wa 's-salaat wa 's-salaam `alaa ashrafi 'l-mursaleen Sayyidina Muhammadin wa `alaa aalihi wa sahbihi ajma`een, then make your *du`a.*

End the Du`a

سُبْحَانَ رَبِّكَ رَبِّ العِزَّةِ عَمَّا يَصِفُونَ وَسَلَامٌ عَلَى المُرْسَلِينَ وَالحَمْدُ لِلَّهِ رَبِّ العَالَمِينَ
ربنا بقبل منا بحرمة من انزلت عليه سورة الفاتحة

Subhaana rabbika rabbi 'l-`izzati `amaa yasifoona wa salaamun `alaa al-mursaleena w'alhamdulillahi rabbi 'l-`alameen. Rabbanaa taqabal minnaa bi hurmati man anzalta `alayhi sirri Suratu 'l-Fatihah.

We learned this *adab* from our guides, Grandshaykh `AbdAllah ق and our master, Mawlana Shaykh Nazim al-Haqqani, may Allah give him long life. On many occasions we saw when Mawlana is reciting his *du`a* it is immediately accepted, as he is pure and his breath is clean with no sin, no *fitna,* no *shirk,* nothing (no flaw)!

Once we were with Mawlana Shaykh Muhammad Nazim ق in Mecca making *tawaaf.* We made the first, the second, the third *tawaaf* and on the fourth we were between *Hajar al-Aswad* and *Baab al Ka'bah,* in that area. *Subhaan-Allah,* it wasn't so crowded and Mawlana ق stopped and stood before *Baab al-Multazam,* saying, "*Bismillahi 'r-Rahmani 'r-Raheem. Alhamdulillahi rabbi 'l-`alameen wa 's-salaat wa 's-salaam `alaa ashrafi 'l-mursaleen Sayyidina Muhammadin wa `alaa aalihi wa sahbihi ajma`een,*" then he began *du`a,* saying, "*Yaa Rabbee,* we came here from a very far place to Your home and we are Your guests, and Your guests await Your *rahmat* and Your *rahmat* is to shower us with it, and the symbol of that *rahmah* is rain, send us rain!" We were at the *Ka'bah* and he was *ilhaa,* being persistent, "Send us rain, send us rain, send us rain, *yaa Rabbee*! You are the Generous," persisting and asking, asking, asking, and people were circumambulating the *Ka'bah,* and then finally he was preparing all this, knocking on the Door, and then finally he said, "For the sake of the Prophet ﷺ, *bi-jaahi 'n-Nabi* ﷺ!" And as soon as he raised his hands and said, "For sake of the Prophet ﷺ," you could see the clouds coming from everywhere. It was really extraordinary and you cannot imagine it! They came from everywhere and when they hit each other thunder came, and you never heard thunder there and it was 40° Centigrade, 120° Fahrenheit, and suddenly it was pouring rain!

In half-an-hour the water was up to the belly, as in that time in the 1960's there was no sewer to take water away, so it was flooded. We had to run to another section in order not to be covered in rain, and you are covered in rain! Before we went up, Mawlana ق went under *Meezaab ar-Rahmat,* that drain pipe from which rainwater flows from the roof of the *Ka'bah.* The Ottomans made it of gold, but before it was wood and in the time of the Prophet ﷺ people used sit there and drink its water or make *wudu* or whatever they wanted to do. We went there with Mawlana ق and drank water from the pipe and then went to another section in order not to be under water. Mecca was completely underwater for six-seven hours and then the water began to slowly, slowly go down.

That is an example of the immediate acceptance of *awliya's du`a* and we are common people, so we have to keep making *du`a* in order that Allah ﷻ will check our patience and then He grants us acceptance!

According to *Al-Jawaab al-Kaafee liman sa'ala `ala' ad-dawaa'i 'sh-shaafee, The Sufficient Answers for Those Who Asked about the Healing Medicine* by Ibn Qayyim al-Jawziyya, the best *du`a* is through the Means of the Prophet ﷺ and through Allah's Beautiful Names and Attributes, and it is not only that:

ورفع يديه إلى الله تعالى وبدأ بحمد الله والثناء عليه ثم ثنى بالصلوة على محمد عبده صلى الله عليه وسلم ثم قدم بين يدي حاجته التوبة والاستغفار ثم دخل على الله والح عليه في المسئلة وتملقه ودعاه رغبة ورهبة وتوسل اليه باسمائه وصفاته وتوحيده

He raises his two hands to Allah and then begins with praising Allah and thanking Him and follows that by salawaat on the Prophet ﷺ, and then he presents his needs in front of Allah then he enters into Allah's Presence, [symbolically through thinking (tafakkur, contemplation) that he is entering the Divine Presence] and then he will insist and persist and ask continuously, showing humility and weakness in front of Allah ﷻ, and he asks Allah, seeking His Pleasure and fearing Him, and he asks intercession for that du`a through Allah's Beautiful Names and Attributes and through His Oneness.

The Importance of Giving Charity to Secure Your Du`a

And now an important point. First you did everything by thanking Allah, praising the Prophet ﷺ asking the means of Prophet, coming to the Divine

Presence, entering and asking through Allah's Beautiful Names and Attributes and through His Oneness, and now the key point:

وقدم بين يدي دعائه صدقة فان هذا الدعاء لا يكاد يرد أبدا

Wa qaddama bayna yaday du`ahi sadaqatan fa inna hadha 'd-du`a laa yakaad yarud abadan.

And in Allah's Divine Presence he presents his du`a with a charity and then he says, "That du`a done in the way that we described, that du`a will never be rejected."

This way *du`a* is accepted immediately and if you give no charity, you don't know if it will be accepted. You have to end it with *sadaqa* and that is why Allah ﷻ said:

خُذْ مِنْ أَمْوَالِهِمْ صَدَقَةً تُطَهِّرُهُمْ وَتُزَكِّيهِم بِهَا وَصَلِّ عَلَيْهِمْ إِنَّ صَلاَتَكَ سَكَنٌ لَّهُمْ وَاللّهُ سَمِيعٌ عَلِيمٌ

Khudh min amwaalihim sadaqatan tutahhiruhum wa tuzakkeehim bihaa wa salli `alayhim inna salaataka sakanun lahum w'Allahu samee`un `aleem.

Take alms of their wealth, from which you may purify them and make them grow, and pray for them. Verily, your prayer is an assuagement for them. Allah is The Hearer, The Knower. *(Surat at-Tawbah, 9:103)*

Finished! If you want something to be done you give *sadaqa*, as Allah ﷻ said, *Khudh min amwaalihim sadaqatan*, "Take from their money a *sadaqa*." You cannot come to the door without a gift; you don't come to someone without a chocolate, something sweet, you don't bring salt. "Take *sadaqa* from them to purify them and clean them," and then it is the responsibility of the Prophet ﷺ to purify and clean them and then pray and ask on their behalf.

You see the procedures? Take *sadaqa* first, make sure that they pay *sadaqa* in any way, but you have to give, then it is the responsibility of the Prophet ﷺ as we see in Holy Qur'an, *tutahhiruhum wa tuzakkeehim*, "to purify them and to clean them," and "then you (Prophet) pray for them, then you ask on their behalf; when they are oppressors to themselves they come to you and you have to ask on their behalf."

وَلَوْ أَنَّهُمْ إِذ ظَّلَمُوا أَنفُسَهُمْ جَآؤُوكَ فَاسْتَغْفَرُوا اللّهَ وَاسْتَغْفَرَ لَهُمُ الرَّسُولُ لَوَجَدُوا اللّهَ تَوَّابًا رَّحِيمًا

Wa law annahum idh zhalamoo anfusahum ja'ooka f 'astaghfaroollaaha w 'astaghfara lahumu 'r-rasoolu la-wajadoo 'Llaaha tawwaaba 'r-raheema.

If they had only, when they were unjust to themselves, come to you and asked Allah's forgiveness, and the Messenger had asked forgiveness for them, they would have found Allah indeed Oft-returning, Most Merciful.

(Surat an-Nisa, 4:64)

"When they are oppressors to themselves, they come to you asking Allah's forgiveness and then you ask forgiveness on their behalf (then it will be accepted)."

So people say, "Why do you repeat an explanation? You keep explaining and explaining." It is like persisting in *du`a*: you say it once and it enters one ear, twice it enters the other ear, three times it enters the heart, say it four times it enters the eyes. So when you take notes of all that we discussed or one line, one sentence when I have discussed five or six sentences, but they say, "What's the point, we can just summarize in one sentence," but in every word of explanation there is a *tajalli* coming, so don't miss even a comma, as the comma is carrying something! Can you omit one letter of the Holy Qur'an? No way! And for *awliyaullah* you cannot omit anything they are saying as you don't know on which word the *tajalli* is coming and the Holy Qur'an is an ocean! The knowledge of all *`ulama* is a drop of that ocean! Listen to why it is an ocean in the following explanation.

It is mentioned in *Sahih Ibn Hibbaan*, narrated from the Hadith:

ثنا عَبْدُ اللَّهِ بْنُ بُرَيْدَةَ ، عَنْ أَبِيهِ رَضِيَ اللَّهُ عَنْهُ ، أَنَّ النَّبِيَّ صَلَّى اللَّهُ عَلَيْهِ وَسَلَّمَ سَمِعَ رَجُلًا ، يَقُولُ : " اللَّهُمَّ إِنِّي أَسْأَلُكَ بِأَنَّكَ أَنْتَ اللَّهُ ، لَا إِلَهَ إِلَّا أَنْتَ الْأَحَدُ الصَّمَدُ ، الَّذِي لَمْ تَلِدْ وَلَمْ تُولَدْ ، وَلَمْ يَكُنْ لَكَ كُفُوًا أَحَدٌ . قَالَ : " لَقَدْ سَأَلْتَ اللَّهَ بِاسْمِهِ الْأَعْظَمِ ، الَّذِي إِذَا سُئِلَ بِهِ أَعْطَى ، وَإِذَا دُعِيَ بِهِ أَجَابَ

From `Abdullah Ibn Buraydah ﷺ that the Prophet ﷺ heard a man say this du`a: "O Allah! I am asking you and witness that you are Allah! There is none to be worshipped except Allah, The Unique that is Not Dependent on Anyone and The One Who does not give birth nor is given birth and there is no one associated with Him." And the Prophet ﷺ said, "Verily he asked Allah by His Greatest Name, that If he asks by that Name he will be granted and if he invokes Allah by it he will be answered."

And what did the Prophet ﷺ say when that person read that *du`a* that we will read it again after this? What did Prophet ﷺ say? "That man has asked Allah ﷻ with His Greatest Name through which if anyone asks Him by that Name it will be given and if he invokes Allah by it He will be answered." So the Greatest Name is hidden there in that *du`a*, so let us repeat it:

> *Allahumma innee asaluka, bi annee ash-hadu annaka anta allahu laa ilaaha illa anta al-ahadu 's-samad, alladhee lam yalid wa lam yulad wa lam yakun lahu kufuwan ahad!*

So what did Prophet say? *Laqad sa'l-allahu bi ismihi 'Lladhee su'ila bihi `u`ud `aata, wa idhaa du`ia bihi ajaab,* and in another narration it says, *Wa laqad sa`alta allahu bi bismihi al-`azham,* "You have asked Allah by His Greatest Name."

And Sayyidina Musa ﷺ asked Allah, "Teach me Your Greatest Name (because the Greatest Name is when you say to a thing, "*Kun fayakoon*! 'Be! and it will be.'"), and Allah said, "No, that is not for you, that is for *Habeebi Muhammad*."

I will mention another Hadith from *Sahih Ibn al-Habban* and in *Sunan Tirmidhi*:

> وفي السنن وصحيح بن حبان أيضا من حديث أنس بن مالك أنه كان مع رسول الله صلى الله عليه وسلم جالسا ورجل يصلى ثم دعا فقال اللهم إني أسالك بأن لك الحمد لا إله الا انت المنان بديع السموات والارض يا ذا الجلال والاكرام يا حى يا قيوم فقال النبي صلى الله عليه وسلم لقد دعا الله باسمه العظيم الذي إذا دعى به أجاب وإذا سئل به

> *Narrated by Anas ibn Malik ﷺ that he was sitting with the Prophet ﷺ and a man was praying, [and for sure that man made a du`a beginning with "Bismillahi 'r-Rahmani 'r-Raheem alhamdulillah rabbi 'l-`alameen wa 's-salaatu wa 's-salaam `alaa ashrafi 'l-mursaleen Sayyidina Muhammadin wa `alaa aalihi wa sahbihi ajma`een,"] and then, "Allahumma innee asaluka bi anna laka al-hamdu la ilaaha illa anta al-mannaanu badi`ee us-samawaati wa 'l-ardi, ya Dhal jalaali wa 'l-ikraam, yaa Hayyu, yaa Qayyum." And the Prophet ﷺ said, verily he has asked Allah by His Greatest Name, if you ask through that Name Allah will respond and if you ask through that Name Allah will give.*

And the Prophet ﷺ said, "He has asked Allah by means of His Greatest Name," and we are asking Allah by His Greatest Name and by the means of Prophet ﷺ, and by means of our *shuyookh*, Sayyidee Shaykh `AbdAllah Fa'iz ad-Daghestani ق and Sayyidee Shaykh Muhammad Nazim al-Haqqani ق to forgive us *an laa tad`a lanaa fee majlisinaa hadha dhamban illa ghafarta wa laa mareedan illa shaafayta wa laa daynan illa qadayta wa laa haajatan min hawaa'ija'd-dunya illa yasartahaa wa qadaytahaa yaa rabbi 'l-`alameen, al-Fatihah.* Give us victory over evil-doing folk and grant us long life to reach the time of Sayyidina al-Mahdi ق and Sayyidina `Isa ﷺ, and we ask Allah the best of what the Prophet ﷺ asked the best of, and we ask protection from the worst of what the Prophet ﷺ asked protection from, and we ask to be with him in this life and the Next and to drink from his Pond a drink after which there is no more thirst, forever!

How very ignorant we are and how much Sahaabah ﷺ with one *du`a* were able to make *du`a* by *Ismullahi l-`Azham*! We are only eating, drinking and sleeping.

May Allah ﷻ forgive us and may Allah ﷻ bless us.

Wa min Allahi 't-tawfiq, bi ḥurmati 'l-ḥabīb, bi ḥurmati 'l-Fātiḥah.

And with Allah is success. For the sake of the Beloved, for his sake we recite the opening chapter of Holy Qur'an.

Special Healing Supplications with Allah's Name

A'ūdhu billāhi min ash-Shayṭāni 'r-rajīm. Bismillāhi' r-Raḥmāni 'r-Raḥīm.
Nawaytu 'l-arbā'īn, nawaytu 'l-'itikāf, nawaytu'l-khalwah, nawaytu 'l-'uzlah,
nawaytu 'r-riyāḍa, nawaytu 's-sulūk, lillāhi Ta'alā fī hādhā 'l-masjid.
Atī'ūllāha wa atī'ū 'r-Rasūla wa ūlī 'l-amri minkum.
Obey Allah, obey the Prophet, and obey those in authority among you. (4:59)

Dastūr, madad yā Sulṭān al-Awlīyā, Mawlana Shaykh Nazim al-Haqqani ق.
Dastūr, madad yā Sulṭān al-Awlīyā, Mawlana Shaykh 'AbdAllah ad-Daghestani ق.

Grandshaykh `AbdAllah ق said that if Allah ﷻ were to expose the reality of a deceased person in his grave, as some have a bad smell—like when making *du`a* part of your *du`a* comes out with a bad smell due to your sins—so if a person dies and Allah ﷻ were to expose the smell of his *gheebah,* backbiting, *nameemah,* false rumors he spread, and his not praying and fasting, his drinking, womanizing, smoking, and the smell of all kinds of actions that Allah ﷻ has forbidden, the whole world would faint! But what about the *du`a* of someone whom Allah ﷻ described in the Holy Qur'an as a pious person, a *wali*? His *du`a* is accepted immediately, as Allah ﷻ said in a Holy Hadith:

من عادا لي وليا فقد آذنته بالحرب

Man `adaa lee waliyyan faqad aadhantahu bi 'l-harb.

(Allah [swt] said) Whoever comes against My wali, I declare war on him.

(Hadith Qudsi; Bukhari, from Abu Hurayrah)

So how will Allah ﷻ declare war against someone whom He described as a *wali*? Allah ﷻ will declare war against the one who comes against His *wali*! That means, *awliyaullah* have no enemies because Allah ﷻ made them pure. That is why the Prophet ﷺ said (that Allah said), "Anyone who comes against a *wali,* I declare war on him," which means that He will accept the *walis' du`as.* Allah will not make war against a *wali.*

You might ask, "Okay, if no one can harm a *wali,* then why do they have problems?" Their problems are not theirs; rather, their problems are like the broadcast camera has a hub and we are carrying our hub and coming to the guide, saying, "We are taking your hand in *baya`* with you." If the guide extends his hand and gives *baya`* to us, then he is responsible for that hub (the harm we all carry) and he has to take it away. So it is our mistakes, our cruelty, our badness and our darkness that we bring to that *wali* that he is carrying for us because he accepted our allegiance to him. so it has become his responsibility to clean us and carry our mistakes. That is why when he makes *du`a* for someone who is coming with all those packages of everything, like laziness or talking too much, the *du`a* will be delayed. It is not because the *wali* is not clean, because they are clean and their *du`a* can be quick, but you have to be clean in order for the *du`a* to reach its place. When you present your situation to him and he makes *du`a*, if you are 90% clean his *du`a* goes like a rocket in order to reach its place and the problem is solved, and if you are 10% clean the speed to reach is reduced by 90%!

That is why Allah ﷻ said in Holy Qur'an:

أَلا إِنَّ أَوْلِيَاء اللّهِ لاَ خَوْفٌ عَلَيْهِمْ وَلاَ هُمْ يَحْزَنُونَ الَّذِينَ آمَنُواْ وَكَانُواْ يَتَّقُونَ

Alaa inna awliyaaullaahi laa khawfun `alayhim wa laa hum yahzanoon. Alladheena amanoo wa kaanoo yattaqoon.

Behold! Verily on the Friends of Allah there is no fear, nor shall they grieve, they who have attained faith and have always been conscious of Him.

(Surat Yunus, 10:62)

The Du`a with Ismullahi 'l-`Azham is Like a Sword

"No fear" means nothing is going to delay their prayers from being accepted, their prayers will be accepted immediately; however, it depends on us and how we come. Any *du`a* you make with *Ismullahi 'l-`Azham*, the Greatest Name of Allah ﷻ, will be like a sword that will cut your problems immediately and bring you towards the Divine Presence! That is why there are *du`as* mentioned by the Sahaabah ؓ that the Prophet ﷺ approved. We can at least take one of these *du`as*, perhaps the easiest one for recitation, learn it and recite it.

There are also other verses of the Holy Qur'an that contain the *Ismullahi 'l-`Azham such as awaa'il as-soowar,* the beginning of all *surahs*. Also, if you read *"Qul huwa Allahu Ahad..."* (*Surat al-Ikhlaas*) three times, it will be as if you have read the whole Qur'an, which means *Ismullahi 'l-`Azham* is included. So the Prophet ﷺ told the Sahaabah ؓ about these *du`as* containing the Greatest Name of Allah and to continue reciting them.

I will read a short one that everyone can learn and recite. As related by Tirmidhi, Asma bint Yazeed ؓ reported the Prophet ﷺ said:

اسْمُ اللَّهِ الأَعْظَمُ فِي هَاتَيْنِ الآيَتَيْنِ : وَإِلَهُكُمْ إِلَهٌ وَاحِدٌ لا إِلَهَ إِلا هُوَ الرَّحْمَنُ الرَّحِيمُ سورة البقرة آية 163 ، وَفَاتِحَةُ سُورَةِ آلِ عِمْرَانَ : الم { 1 } اللَّهُ لا إِلَهَ إِلا هُوَ الْحَيُّ الْقَيُّومُ { 2 } سورة آل عمران آية 1-2 ."

Allah's Greatest Name is in these two verses: Wa ilaahukum ilaahun waahidun laa ilaaha illa Huwa 'r-Rahmaanu 'r-Raheem, "And your God is one God: there is no god but He, the Compassionate, the Merciful." (Surat al-Baqara, 2:163), and the beginning of Al-`Imraan (3:1-2): Alif. Laam. Meem. Allaahu laa ilaaha illa Huwa 'l-Hayyu 'l- Qayyum. Alif. Laam. Meem. "Allah, there is no god but He, the Ever-Living, the Eternal."

(Tirmidhi, Abu Dawud, Ibn Majah, and Darimi)

And all of you know these two verses: *wa ilaahukum ilaahun waahidun laa ilaaha illa Huwa 'r-Rahmaanu 'r-Raheem*, and, *Alif. Laam. Meem. Allaahu laa ilaaha illa Huwa 'l-Hayyu 'l- Qayyum*; one from *Surat al-Baqara* and one from *Al-`Imraan*. Anyone who has a problem and makes *du`a* through these two verses that contain *Ismullahi l-`Azham*, Allah ﷻ will accept what he wants!

حديث أبي هريرة - رضي الله عنه - أن النبي - صلى الله عليه وسلم - كان إذا أهمه الأمر رفع رأسه إلى السماء ، وإذا اجتهد في الدعاء ، قال : يا حي يا قيوم .

Anna 'n-Nabi ﷺ kaana idhaa ahamahu 'l-amra rafa`a raasahu ila 's-samaa wa idhaa 'jtahada fi 'd-du`aa, qaala: Ya Hayyu Yaa Qayyum.

As related by Abu Hurayrah ؓ, whenever a burden or a difficult matter came on him, the Prophet ﷺ would raise his head towards the sky and when he strove hard in invocation, he would say, "Yaa Hayyu, yaa Qayyum!"

(Sahih Tirmidhi)

Usually we look at our hands when making *du`a*, but when there is a big affliction, rather than showing humbleness you raise our hands high, saying, *"Yaa Rabbee! Yaa Rabbee!"* to show that you are really in need. So the Prophet ﷺ raised his hands, looked toward the Heavens and said, *"Yaa Hayyu, yaa Qayyum! Yaa Hayyu, yaa Qayyum! Yaa Hayyu, yaa Qayyum! Yaa*

Hayyu, yaa Qayyum! Yaa bad`ee as-samawaati wa 'l-ardh, yaa Dhu 'l-Jalaali wa 'l-Ikraam." When you say it like this Allah ﷻ will accept your *du'a*.

من حديث أنس بن مالك ، قال : كان النبي - صلى الله عليه وسلم - إذا حزبه أمر قال : يا حي يا قيوم برحمتك أستغيث.

Kaan an-Nabi ﷺ idhaa hazabahu amran qaala:Yaa Hayyu, yaa Qayyum! Bi-rahmatika astagheeth.

As related by Anas bin Malik ؓ, whenever the Prophet ﷺ went into a difficulty he raised his hands and said, "Yaa Hayyu, yaa Qayyum! Bi-rahmatika astagheeth, O Living One! O Established One! With Your Mercy I seek Your help! Accept from me!" (Sahih Tirmidhi)

Finally, I will mention the "*Du`a* of Yunus" that Sayyidina Yunus ؑ recited when he was inside the stomach of a whale.

وفي جامع الترمذي وصحيح الحاكم من حديث سعد بن أبي وقاص عن النبي - صلى الله عليه وسلم - قال : دعوة ذي النون ، إذ دعا وهو في بطن الحوت " لا إله إلا أنت سبحانك إني كنت من الظالمين [سورة الأنبياء : 87] إنه لم يدع بها مسلم في شيء قط إلا استجاب الله له . قال الترمذي : حديث صحيح

`An an-Nabi ﷺ qaala: da`wata dhi'n-noon, idh da`a wa huwa fee butooni'l-hoot "laa ilaha illa anta subhaanak innee kuntu min azh-zhaalimeen." innahu lam yad`u bihaa Muslim fee shayyin qat illa'stajaab allahu lahu.

The Prophet ﷺ said, "The supplication of my brother Dhun Nun (Yunus) ؑ, who called on Allah while in the whale's belly: 'There is no god but You. Glory be to You! Verily, I have been among the wrongdoers.' (Surat al-Anbiya 21:87) No Muslim person says it for any situation whatsoever except that Allah Most High answers his call." (Tirmidhi)

When Sayyidina Yunus ؑ was unhappy with his people, Allah ﷻ sent him to a village with a population of 100,000 people. No one believed in him, so he ran away and stopped delivering the Message. To teach him a lesson, Allah ﷻ sent a whale to swallow him. That whale was able to cut him to pieces, but it didn't, as Allah ﷻ saves a *mu'min* from difficulties. Don't come and say, "I have problems." Everyone has problems, but as we just mentioned, when the Prophet ﷺ had problems he raised his hands and said, "*Yaa Hayyu, yaa Qayyum! Bi-rahmaatika astagheeth.*" You are not better than him ﷺ! So Sayyidina Yunus (as) was reciting in the whale *"laa ilaha illa anta subhaanak innee kuntu min azh-zhaalimeen."*

Problems come in order to purify and reward you and to raise your station higher and higher, but this depends on how patient you are: with your father, your mother, your Prophet ﷺ, and with the tests coming from your guide. Allah ﷻ is patient! The last of His Ninety-Nine Names is *as-Saboor*, The Most Patient One," which comes after strong and heavy names such as *al-Jabbar* and *al-Qahhar*. Through this, Allah ﷻ is telling us, "I am *as-Saboor*, the Patient One." Why is He patient? He used to destroy nations, flip them up and down and send down stones from Hellfire! Allah ﷻ sent these stones or comets on Earth from Hellfire, which means *Jahannam* is everywhere as they are coming from just above the atmosphere, not from four-billion light years away. This also means there is punishment everywhere, but why isn't Allah sending them, why is He patient with us? He is patient because of His Love to the Prophet ﷺ and his *ummah*, and for whose sake Allah ﷻ forgave the *ummah*! Don't think you are living happily and that Allah ﷻ is providing you everything due to your goodness! No, we are not good; rather, (He is saving us) because of one verse in the Holy Qur'an:

قل لَا أَسْأَلُكُمْ عَلَيْهِ أَجْرًا إِلَّا الْمَوَدَّةَ فِي الْقُرْبَى

Qul laa as'alukum `alayhi ajran illa al-mawaddata fi 'l-qurbah.
Say (O Muhammad), "I do not ask you for a reward except the love of my family." (Surat ash-Shura, 42:23)

Allah ﷻ loves you because He loves the Prophet ﷺ, who loves his *Ahlu 'l-Bayt*! *Ahlu 'l-Bayt* are of two kinds: the whole *ummah*, since we are from *Ummat an-Nabi* ﷺ, and the Family of the Prophet ﷺ, the core or real ones who are at the center of the circle. The Prophet ﷺ is the center of the circle while his *ummah* are around the circumference receiving from the center that gives millions of thin radii to the circumference. The Prophet ﷺ, along with his *Ahlu 'l-Bayt*, are in the circle. Who is under the *abaya*, cloak of the Prophet ﷺ, who was under the jubbah of the Prophet ﷺ when he put it on? Let's begin from the youngest: Sayyidina al-Husayn ؓ, Sayyidina al-Hasan ؓ, Sayyidina Fatima az-Zahra ؓ, Sayyidina `Ali ؓ and Sayyidina Muhammad ﷺ—these five are from *Ahlu 'l-Bayt* and the rest are their direct descendants, all of whom are in the center and the others are on the circumference. So for the love of the Prophet ﷺ, Allah ﷻ saved the whole circle, the center and the circumference!

Allah ﷻ has patience with you until you die, and He says, "If you ask for forgiveness, at that time I will grant it to you, don't worry!" But don't come like people today with all kinds of sins. Today, children are not listening to their parents. Allah wants you to listen to your parents! Parents also disobey Allah ﷻ because they say, "This is the New Year (so let's celebrate)." Every moment of your life is a New Year, not just those two or three days! Since bad people celebrate the New Year by drinking and womanizing, we must avoid being in the middle of that. You don't need to go out and be dressed with the darkness of that night; instead, sit at home and make *istighfaar* after *Salaat al-`Isha*. Sit and eat with your family and don't go out, don't be part of it. You can go to visit your parents or children, but don't celebrate as they celebrate by drinking and so on. Be careful! You don't know, like when Allah ﷻ was sending comets on `Ad and Thamud, they sent every good one (away) from the village with Sayyidina Lut ؑ because if they had left them there they would have also been destroyed!

May Allah ﷻ forgive us and may Allah ﷻ bless us.

Wa min Allahi 't-tawfīq, bi ḥurmati 'l-ḥabīb, bi ḥurmati 'l-Fātiḥah.

And with Allah is success. For the sake of the Beloved, for his sake we recite the opening chapter of Holy Qur'an.

The Supplication of Sayyidina Yunus

A'ūdhu billāhi min ash-Shayṭāni 'r-rajīm. Bismillāhi' r-Raḥmāni 'r-Raḥīm. Nawaytu 'l-arbā'īn, nawaytu 'l-'itikāf, nawaytu'l-khalwah, nawaytu 'l-'uzlah, nawaytu 'r-riyāḍa, nawaytu 's-sulūk, lillāhi Ta'alā fī hādhā 'l-masjid. Atī'ūllāha wa atī'ū 'r-Rasūla wa ūlī 'l-amri minkum.
Obey Allah, obey the Prophet, and obey those in authority among you. (4:59)

Dastūr, madad yā Sulṭān al-Awlīyā, Mawlana Shaykh Nazim al-Haqqani ق.
Dastūr, madad yā Sulṭān al-Awlīyā, Mawlana Shaykh 'AbdAllah ad-Daghestani ق.

Alhamdulillah that Allah ﷻ with His *Karam*, Generosity, gave us life, and how many children die in the womb of the mother? Allah ﷻ not only gave us life, but on top of that He made us from *Ummat an-Nabi* ﷺ! It is *ummatan marhooma*, the *ummah* blessed with Allah's Mercy, and *ummatan maghfoorah*, an *ummah* that Allah has forgiven. And there are many *ahadith* on that, which is not our discussion today. So in order that Allah ﷻ forgives us from our sins, He mentioned to us through His beloved Prophet ﷺ to read from Holy Qur'an.

Imagine this: they do statistics for publishing houses, for example there are hundreds of books and (they do statistics to see) how many people have read them and which has the highest percentage of (readership), is it not? And the one with highest percentage becomes the favorite. And so you see hundreds of people rush to buy it and read it, because too many people have read that and are happy with it. And I heard that the most-read book which also made the most money is *Harry Potter*, and that it is not just millions who have read it, but hundreds of millions have read it, and they made millions of copies and Muslims and non-Muslims have read it. Is that right? And they made a movie out of it and you have to stand in line for hours and hours to go inside the movie theater, Muslims and non-Muslims alike. People were happy with that author, a young lady, and the author was happy because everyone was reading her book.

So let us ask ourselves about that *Harry Potter* book. It is imaginary and not worth nickels or pennies, even five cents is too much, or not worth reading because it is a waste of time, but people are jumping to get it, and you have to place an order to get that book as it is not available. And then you keep reading and they ask you questions in school and ask you to write an essay from it and it becomes a project. And everyone is rushing to read it over and over in order to understand it more, and what did you get at the end? They took your money! Is there anything else?

There is not one single book in the whole world that if you read it they gave you money, is there? Only one book, that if you read it you get wealth in *dunya* and *Akhirah*! And not only that, but Allah ﷻ will be very happy with you because of you reading His Divine Words that are the Holy Qur'an and there are *ahadith* of Prophet ﷺ. Ask all *`ulama* around, even scholars who write books, and there are many scholars who write books on many issues that concern Muslims, but not concerning *Akhirah* issues, for example, on banking in Islam, psychology of Muslim identity and many other topics, but these authors still take your money and if you read their books you will still not be rewarded. But if you read *Hadith an-Nabi* ﷺ and Holy Qur'an, you get wealth in *dunya* and *Akhirah, shifaa'* in *dunya* and *Akhirah*, rewards in *dunya* and *Akhirah*, happiness in *dunya* and *Akhirah*, blessings in *dunya* and *Akhirah* and you will be with the Prophet ﷺ in *dunya* and *Akhirah*, and you will be able to see Allah ﷻ in Paradise! Is there any other book that can do that other than Holy Qur'an and Hadith of the Prophet ﷺ? Show them to me! Why then is the Holy Qur'an left on shelves and *ahadith* of the Prophet ﷺ are only on shelves?

Mercy and Healing for Those Who Read Holy Qur'an

If you don't know Arabic, you can at least look at the pages. Open the page, put your finger at the first *ayah* and keep moving along the lines. If you don't know how to read, try to learn. Pakistanis know how to read Urdu, it is written in Arabic script, the Persians also have Arabic script, they have no excuse, the Bengalis might have an excuse and those in India also might not know how to read Arabic, but Urdu-speaking people have no excuse and Arabs absolutely have no excuse, they will be asked! May Allah ﷻ not ask us and send us to Paradise with no questions. And if this whole *dunya* came together to read and to reward you for their books, and you are reading the Holy Qur'an, their reward means nothing compared to Allah's Rewards. Allah will reward us from His Greatness that has no beginning and no end, and will He reward us from His Mercy that has no beginning and no end!

يَا أَيُّهَا النَّاسُ قَدْ جَاءَتْكُم مَّوْعِظَةٌ مِّن رَّبِّكُمْ وَشِفَاءٌ لِّمَا فِي الصُّدُورِ وَهُدًى وَرَحْمَةٌ لِّلْمُؤْمِنِينَ

Mankind there has come to you a guidance from your Lord and a healing for (the diseases) in your hearts, and for those who believe a guidance and a mercy. (Surat Yunus, 10:57)

When you read the *Harry Potter* books, do you get cured? Read it a hundred times, is there any cure? You get disturbed even more! There is no comparison from all *dunya* books to the Holy Qur'an; that one is *dunya* words and this one is Allah's Words, so everything else is Shaytan's words if it is not Hadith or Islamic books, so you must run to it! On every letter of the Holy Qur'an there are Allah's Rewards; not only on every word, but on every letter that you recite, because a letter is like the abbreviations *"Alif. Laam. Meem."* or *"Kaaf. Haa. Yaa. `Ayn. Saad."* at the beginning of many *surahs*, three, four or five letters, and you don't know their meanings, but these are secret encrypted letters of words of Holy Qur'an. Every letter is divine and has rewards. So from the number of letters in a word, for example, it is four, they are the divine letters that comprise the words of the Holy Qur'an. Take any letter you want, as in the word "Allah," every letter is divine: in *"ar-Rahman,"* every letter is divine as it is part of the word.

Not one book from around the world gives you reward when you read it except the Holy Qur'an, and for reading even one letter, Allah ﷻ will reward you as He said:

وَنُنَزِّلُ مِنَ الْقُرْآنِ مَا هُوَ شِفَاءٌ وَرَحْمَةٌ لِّلْمُؤْمِنِينَ

Wa nunazzilu mina al-qur'ani ma huwa shifaa'un wa rahmatun li 'l-mu'mineen.

And We sent down in the Qur'an such things that have healing and mercy for the believers. (Surat al-'Israa, 17:82)

"We revealed and sent down what is a cure for believers." Since the beginning of *surahs* have encrypted letters, it means every letter in Holy Qur'an has *shifaa'* in it. So which (*dunya*) book can give *shifaa'*? There is none, no way! It is (only) the Holy Qur'an. Good tidings to you *mu'mins* and Muslims, that Allah ﷻ gave you the Holy Qur'an that will take all your problems and give you happiness, and Allah accepts from you, even if you have done something wrong, if you ask forgiveness Allah will forgive you!

Allah ﷻ sent Sayyidina Yunus ؑ to 100,000 people to call them to Him. He called and called, and they didn't listen to him and so he ran away (seeking solitude in Allah). What happened to him? Allah taught him a lesson and He ordered the whale to swallow him. What did Sayyidina Yunus ؑ do? Look at the *barakah* of the Holy Qur'an! In *Jami`ah at-Tirmidhi* and the *Sahih al-Hakim*, Sa`d Ibn Abi Waqqas ؓ said that Sayyidina Yunus ؑ used to make a *du`a* in the belly of the whale that is a verse in Holy Qur'an:

لَّا إِلَٰهَ إِلَّا أَنتَ سُبْحَانَكَ إِنِّي كُنتُ مِنَ الظَّالِمِينَ

Laa ilaaha illa Anta! Subhaanaka innee kuntu min azh-zhaalimeen!

There is no god except You! Limitless are You in Your Glory! Verily, I am among the oppressors! (Surat al-Anbiya, 21:87)

Is it Holy Qur'an or not? "O Allah! There is no one except You and I was an oppressor to myself," because he ran away and did not continue (the order to deliver the Message). So what did the Prophet ﷺ say? *Annahu lam yadu`a bihi shayin Muslim qat illa yastajib lahu*, "In anything that you ask, in illness or need, or anything at all, if you recite that verse Allah will respond to you and answer you." But Sayyidina Yunus ؑ didn't say it only once, he was saying it continuously on his breathing in and breathing out, until Allah's test finished and the whale threw him out.

Is there any book other than Holy Qur'an that you recite or read from and the Prophet ﷺ will say if you ask Allah through it, like that verse of Holy Qur'an that Sayyidina Yunus ؑ was saying, you get acceptance or reward? No way. And that verse is part of the Holy Qur'an. That means the Holy Qur'an is the book you get rewarded for reading every time and in each reading rewarded a different way. For example, if you read *Surat al-Baqara* from beginning to end you will get reward, and if you read it the next day, don't think the reward will be the same as for the first reading. If you read it a third time the reward is different, and each time you read the same *surah* there is different reward and a different *tajalli* coming on you on that day.

That is why some Sahaabah ؓ used to read the whole Holy Qur'an in one day, including the night. It takes twenty minutes to read one *juz* (one-thirtieth), so thirty *juz* can be finished in six-hundred minutes, which is ten hours, or some people can read them in fifteen hours. There are some people who don't stop (read continuously). The *muqrieen*, those who (memorized) and recite Holy Qur'an, have principles in reciting the Holy

Qur'an and every day they have to recite five *juz* to keep refreshing their memory. So Allah is telling us, recite it like Dhul-Nun, Sayyidina Yunus, recite, *"Laa ilaaha illa Anta! Subhaanaka innee kuntu min azh-zhalimeen,"* and you will get reward from Him in health and wealth. Say it and get the reward!

We mentioned many *du`as* yesterday that have *Ismullah al-`Azham* in them. Sayyidina Anas heard someone asking, "Do you want me to tell you about the Greatest Name?" and Sayyidina Musa was asking Allah to teach him that Greatest Name, which, if you use it, Allah will grant whatever you ask immediately without restriction!

The Prophet asked the Sahaabah, "Do you want me to teach you the Greatest Name of Allah? It is the *du`a* of Sayyidina Yunus." One man asked, "Is that private to Yunus?" and the Prophet said, "Did you not hear Allah's Word?"

فَاسْتَجَبْنَا لَهُ وَنَجَّيْنَاهُ مِنَ الْغَمِّ وَكَذَلِكَ نُنجي الْمُؤْمِنِينَ

Fastajabnaa lahu wa najaynaahu min al-ghamm wa kadhaalika nunjee 'l-mu'mineen.

And so We responded to him and delivered him from his distress, for thus do We deliver all who have faith. (Surat al-Anbiya, 21:88)

It means, "We accepted his *du`a* and We saved him from all *ghamm*, miseries!" So if you read the Holy Qur'an it will save you, and any Muslim or *mu'min* who recites this verse during his illness from which he dies, if he recited it forty times then he will die as a *shaheed*. *Allahu Akbar*! People were running to die as *shaheed* (martyr) in the time of the Prophet. When Prophet declared there is a war to defend Muslims from aggression, as he defended his people through holy wars, and Allah gave them *ajar shaheed*. And the Prophet said, "If you recite this verse forty times and die on your bed, you will be given the reward of a *shaheed*! *Wa in buriya buriya maghfooran lah*, and if he didn't die he will be cured and he will be forgiven."

So let us try to recite it now to get cured as there is no holy war now; the holy war has principles and (currently) they are not there, but when Mahdi comes that is different. But now if you recite it you will get a cure and you will be forgiven. *Laa ilaaha illa Anta! Subhaanaka innee kuntu min azh-zhaalimeen fastajabnaa lahu wa najaynaahu min al-ghamm wa kadhaalika nunjee 'l-mu'mineen.*

That is the only book that gives that reward, so don't put it on the shelves, put it in your hearts, which means to read it. If we don't know how to read, *awliyaullah* gave a *fatwa* for those who don't know (that they may look at the Arabic words), but we know how to read and we have to try as much as possible to read. May Allah ﷻ forgive us for not giving the Holy Qur'an it's rights! But for those who are converts and don't know how to read, they have to put their finger under the *ayah* and move it and read the commentary on the side so at least they will know what they are reading and understand the meaning.

And Allah ﷻ is Great! He knows we cannot read, so Allah ﷻ will still reward us. May Allah ﷻ forgive us, bless us, reward us and cure us and give us health and wealth in *dunya* and *Akhirah* and forgiveness *bi jaahi 'l-qur'an,* for the sake of the Holy Qur'an.

May Allah ﷻ forgive us and may Allah ﷻ bless us.

Wa min Allahi 't-tawfiq, bi ḥurmati 'l-ḥabīb, bi ḥurmati 'l-Fātiḥah.

And with Allah is success. For the sake of the Beloved, for his sake we recite the opening chapter of Holy Qur'an.

Holy Qur'an is the Only Book that Gives and Does Not Take

A'ūdhu billāhi min ash-Shayṭāni 'r-rajīm. Bismillāhi' r-Raḥmāni 'r-Raḥīm.
Nawaytu 'l-arbā'īn, nawaytu 'l-'itikāf, nawaytu'l-khalwah, nawaytu 'l-'uzlah,
nawaytu 'r-riyāḍa, nawaytu 's-sulūk, lillāhi Ta'alā fī hādhā 'l-masjid.
Atī'ūllāha wa atī'ū 'r-Rasūla wa ūlī 'l-amri minkum.
Obey Allah, obey the Prophet, and obey those in authority among you. (4:59)

Dastūr, madad yā Sulṭān al-Awlīyā, Mawlana Shaykh Nazim al-Haqqani ق.
Dastūr, madad yā Sulṭān al-Awlīyā, Mawlana Shaykh 'AbdAllah ad-Daghestani ق.

O Muslims! O Believers! These days many people are busy trying to observe something that is truly an innovation. Some *`ulama* say that observing the Prophet's birthday is an innovation, while other (scholarly) opinions say it's not and they celebrate by remembering and observing the *Seerah* and *Mawlid* of the Prophet ﷺ. In any case, we are not going to discuss this now, about which we can show it is in fact acceptable in Islam, but we want to touch on another issue that is the real innovation practiced by Muslims and non-Muslims alike.

وَالنَّجْمِ إِذَا هَوَى مَا ضَلَّ صَاحِبُكُمْ وَمَا غَوَى وَمَا يَنطِقُ عَنِ الْهَوَى إِنْ هُوَ إِلَّا وَحْيٌ يُوحَى

By the star when it goes down, your Companion is neither astray nor being misled, nor does he say (aught) of (his own) desire. It is no less than inspiration sent down to him. *(Surat an-Najm, 53:1-4)*

Why do they come against the Prophet's ﷺ birthday when they don't come against Sayyidina Isa's ﷺ birthday? Allah ﷻ said in the Holy Qur'an about Sayyidina `Isa ﷺ:

وَالسَّلَامُ عَلَيَّ يَوْمَ وُلِدْتُ وَيَوْمَ أَمُوتُ وَيَوْمَ أُبْعَثُ حَيًّا

Peace be upon me the day I was born, the day I will die, and the day I will be resurrected. *(Surat al-Maryam, 19:33)*

Similarly, for Sayyidina Yahya ؑ, when Allah ﷻ gave Sayyidina Zakariyya ؑ a son, He said:

$$وَسَلَامٌ عَلَيْهِ يَوْمَ وُلِدَ وَيَوْمَ يَمُوتُ وَيَوْمَ يُبْعَثُ حَيًّا$$

So peace on him the day he was born, the day that he dies, and the day that he will be raised up to life (again)! (Surat Maryam, 19:15)

Today we are seeing people celebrating Sayyidina `Isa's ؑ birthday, even Muslims, when on the other hand they say it's bida` for our Prophet, Sayyidina Muhammad ﷺ! I saw that with my own eyes in New York when I was invited to a Muslim's house and there were many scholars there. I saw a big Christmas tree at the corner of the big room, as he was a rich person.

I said, "What is this?"

He said, "O Shaykh! No problem, it's okay."

I said, "No, I don't mind, as Allah ﷻ mentioned in the Holy Qur'an (about Sayyidina `Isa), *wa 's-salaamu `alayya yawma wulidtu wa yawma amootu wa yawma ub`athu hayyaan*. But for what reason are you putting (a Christmas tree)?"

He said, "For the children."

Many people sitting there didn't say anything, although some of them didn't like that there was a Christmas tree.

I asked the children, "What you are celebrating?"

They said, "Jesus's birthday."

I said, "Who is your Prophet?"

They said, "Muhammad ﷺ."

So I asked, "Do you know when he was born?" and they didn't know. Then I asked, "Do you know when Jesus was born?"

They said, "December 25th!"

So unfortunately, there is no education about Islam, which is why people are now celebrating the New Year on 1 January, but that is not our New Year. Which New Year must we celebrate, the Christian New Year or the Hijri New Year (1 Muharram)? The Hijri New Year! How many of us celebrated the Hijri New Year? Today everyone is celebrating the Christian New Year. I am not blaming anyone, but we have to be careful of what we teach ourselves and our children. How many read the Harry Potter books? Most of you. Did Harry Potter take money from you or did you gave him money? We gave him money and we gave him importance and read his book and made our children to read that book. That lady, the author of the Harry Potter books, takes billions of dollars!

Everyone's book takes money from you, it does not give you except one book, and if you keep that book you will be wealthy and healthy! If you keep that book in your heart you will be happy in *dunya* and *Akhirah*! It is the only book that can give you back rewards and nothing else! No other book can give you rewards except any book connected to that main book. All other books are human beings' writing. Holy Qur'an is Allah's Divine Knowledge, *Kalaamullah al-Qadeem*, Allah's Ancient Words! Every letter of Holy Qur'an is, by itself, a universe of rewards that Allah gives you and it is the book that gives everyone happiness!

Go to the pharmacy; how many medicines and drugs do they have there? Thousands! They say, "This is for that benefit and that is for this," and what do they do? They take your money and they tell you it benefits you but it has a side effect that might make you worse! The only one that doesn't make you worse is the Holy Qur'an:

يَا أَيُّهَا النَّاسُ قَدْ جَاءتْكُم مَّوْعِظَةٌ مِّن رَّبِّكُمْ وَشِفَاء لِّمَا فِي الصُّدُورِ وَهُدًى وَرَحْمَةٌ لِّلْمُؤْمِنِينَ

Mankind there has come to you a guidance from your Lord and a healing for (the diseases) in your hearts and for those who believe a guidance and a mercy.

(Surat Yunus, 10:57)

O Human Beings! Allah is giving you remedies! Every word and verse of Holy Qur'an is a remedy for your *dunya* and *Akhirah*! Even if you put it on the shelf you will get rewarded and if you read it you get more reward, and every time you read it you get a different reward than the first time and it doesn't stay the same!

What are rewards? Rewards are levels or ascensions in Paradise. Every reward is an ascension in Paradise, in *Akhirah*! Every letter, word and verse of Holy Qur'an is divine! Allah ﷻ said, "This is My Book! Read it, it will heal you spiritually and physically."

O Muslims! On that night of 31st December, don't go out of the house like other people because the *shayateen* are everywhere, drinking in the streets and womanizing, doing all kinds of *haraam*, jumping, dancing and

Qawmi Loot, gay people are everywhere. And Allah's Curse with come! Don't go out that night, but stay home and read Holy Qur'an; invite your friend and read Holy Qur'an and Hadith of Prophet ﷺ. Allah will see you are sitting, staying home with your family and remembering Him!

May Allah open our hearts to the love of Holy Qur'an and just as we are coming to pray, we need to also open the Holy Qur'an and read. Some people might say they don't know how to read, but never mind, but at least open the Holy Qur'an and if you don't know how to read, try to learn to read Arabic and if you cannot, at least move your finger under the words and read the meaning in different languages, as this way at least you show respect for Holy Qur'an.

May Allah make it for us *shafaa`* on Judgment Day and in the grave a light, and may it cure us in *dunya* and take away from us our problems!

When you delay reading Shaytan is playing so step over that and read! Shaytan comes in all different ways to stop you from reading Holy Qur'an. Sometimes I am reading and all kinds of telephone calls come in order to stop you reading. Don't stop, simply close your phone and don't answer it, except if you have guests and have to take care of them it is okay, or if you are sick or traveling it is okay. However, try your best to not abandon reading Holy Qur'an, even read one page or just *"Bismillahi 'r-Rahmani 'r-Raheem"* and the first *ayah* of the surah, but don't leave Holy Qur'an sitting on the shelf.

May Allah ﷻ forgive us and may Allah ﷻ bless us.

Wa min Allahi 't-tawfiq, bi ḥurmati 'l-ḥabīb, bi ḥurmati 'l-Fātiḥah.

And with Allah is success. For the sake of the Beloved, for his sake we recite the opening chapter of Holy Qur'an.

Supplication for Calamity and the Adab of Du`a

A'ūdhu billāhi min ash-Shayṭāni 'r-rajīm. Bismillāhi' r-Raḥmāni 'r-Raḥīm. Nawaytu 'l-arbā'īn, nawaytu 'l-'itikāf, nawaytu'l-khalwah, nawaytu 'l-'uzlah, nawaytu 'r-riyāḍa, nawaytu 's-sulūk, lillāhi Ta'alā fī hādhā 'l-masjid. Atī'ūllāha wa atī'ū 'r-Rasūla wa ūlī 'l-amri minkum. Obey Allah, obey the Prophet, and obey those in authority among you. (4:59)

Dastūr, madad yā Sulṭān al-Awlīyā, Mawlana Shaykh Nazim al-Haqqani ق.
Dastūr, madad yā Sulṭān al-Awlīyā, Mawlana Shaykh 'AbdAllah ad-Daghestani ق.

As we mentioned previously, Allah ﷻ revealed in the Holy Qur'an that He sent Holy Qur'an as *shifaa'*, cure for humanity and He said that there is no differentiation for humanity, but others differentiate. Allah sent Sayyidina Muhammad ﷺ for the entire world! It is their problem that they did not accept Islam and align themselves and then on the Day of Judgment they cannot say, "We didn't hear or see the verses of Holy Qur'an or *du`as* that cure physical and spiritual sicknesses."

وَنُنَزِّلُ مِنَ الْقُرْآنِ مَا هُوَ شِفَاء وَرَحْمَةٌ لِّلْمُؤْمِنِينَ

Wa nunazzilu mina al-qur'ani maa huwa shifaa'un wa rahmatan li 'l-mu'mineen.

And We sent down in the Qur'an such things that have healing and mercy for the believers. *(Surat al-'Israa, 17:82)*

Spiritual sicknesses are more difficult to cure because you cannot easily diagnose the illness as it requires very highly qualified spiritual guides. There are too many specialists for physical illness who can diagnose not all, but many sicknesses and through their own studies they can give you something that can make you feel better. This is a means, *waseelah*, that Allah gave to doctors to do their best as we know that the cure comes from Allah, whether physical or spiritual. That is why Holy Qur'an can, for sure, cure physical and spiritual illnesses.

Allah ﷻ said, "We sent down in the Qur'an such things that have healing and mercy for the believers," spiritual or physical, so we must follow what Allah said with belief. The one guiding you to that must believe in what he is saying, and the one receiving must also believe that the verse or *du'a* the guide is giving is going to heal them; it is not that one, but it is Allah who heals you through these verses or du'as. Allah ﷻ gave *awliyaullah* the authority to heal. We have been discussing this in this series of lectures, now we are on the eighth. It would be best to start from the beginning to better understand this idea.

Most of the Sahaabah ؓ and those who came after were using spiritual means of Holy Qur'an through His verses, as they are Allah's Words. When you mention Allah's Words, for example, saying, *"Ash-hadu an laa ilaaha illa-Llah, wa ash-hadu anna Muhammadan `abduhu wa habeebuhu wa rasooluh,"* and, *"`alayhaa nahya wa `alayhaa namoot wa `alayhaa nalqa-Allah,"* upon waking up in the morning and then making *wudu* and brushing your teeth, we do this so as to make them clean and to make us feel nice. This means that Allah's Words make us feel nice, but our belief is weak. We often ask our children in the morning or evening if they brushed their teeth and we expect them to brush their teeth in order not to get cavities. So why then are you not brushing your mind and heart in order not to get cavities in your heart for Shaytan to come through? (Speaking to a doctor) Why don't you tell your patients to brush their teeth by reciting Holy Qur'an in the morning and to say, *"Ash-hadu an laa ilaaha illa-Llah, wa ash-hadu anna Muhammadan `abduhu wa habeebuhu wa rasooluh."* If not, then there will be too many cavities in the heart and mind that Shaytan may come through and that is the illness of the spirit.

Shaytan Enters a Weak Area and Brings Disease

We know now that DNA is the blueprint for every Creation and in that blueprint there are doors and windows that are accessible for Shaytan to enter. If he enters from Door X, you may get sickness X; if he enters from Door Y, you may get sickness Y; if he enters from Door A, you may get AIDS. There some doors that are not as dangerous in comparison to those that are *maradaat al-jinn*, but you may get an illness that is impossible to cure or heal. Why do they do chemotherapy? Because Shaytan enters the body and spreads that illness, making that smell spread throughout the entire body.

So we must believe what Prophet ﷺ said:

قال رسول الله : لكل داء دواء فإذا أصاب دواء الداء برأ بإذن الله.

Li kulli daa'in dawaa fa idhaa asaaba dawaa ad-da'aa baraa bi-idhnillah.

For every illness there is a cure. So if the cure is applied to the illness, it will be removed by Allah's Will.

And the Prophet ﷺ said:

ما أنزل اللهُ مِنْ داءٍ إلا أنْزَلَ لهُ شِفَاءً علمه من علمه وجهله من جهله

Maa anzal-Allahu min daa'in illa anzala lahu shifaa'an; `alamahu man `alamahu wa jahalahu man jahalahu.

Allah did not send down a sickness except He sent down with it a cure. He who knows it, knows it and he who is ignorant of it is ignorant of it.

(Abu Hurayrah in Sahih Bukhari)

And that cure is not through drugs. With one-million percent certainty that cure will come from Holy Qur'an, because Allah ﷻ said:

فإذا قرأتَ القُرْآنَ فاسْتَعِذْ باللهِ مِنَ الشَّيْطانِ الرَّجيم

Fa idhaa qiraat al-qur`an fasta`idh billaahi min ash-shaytani 'r-rajeem.

When you read the Holy Qur'an, you must ask support from Allah against Shaytan, the Accursed. *(Surat an-Nahl, 16:98)*

Blocking the Weak Entry Point

When you seek refuge and say, *"A`oodhu billahi min ash-Shaytaani 'r-rajeem,"* all these cavities will be blocked and Shaytan will be unable to enter. If Shaytan enters, you may get the sickness that corresponds to the door he entered from. That is why there are compilations of hundreds and thousands of *du`a al-maa'thooraat,* Prophet's recommended *du`a* that shuts these doors. People think they get sicknesses from this disease or that, but in reality it is from wherever Shaytan enters. You may have been *ghaafil,* heedless, and he was able to enter through that entrance and throw different diseases through that door.

There are young *shaytan*, teen-aged *shaytan*, adult *shaytan,* and old *shaytan*. Unlike *jinn*, they don't die except in the end. *Maradat al-Jinn* are the worst *shaytans* and they don't die, whereas normal *jinn* marry, have children and die. So be careful of Shaytan! Allah ﷻ said to recite, *"A`oodhu billahi min ash-Shaytaani 'r-rajeem. Bismillahi 'r-Rahmaani 'r-Raheem"* before reading

Holy Qur'an. Why is it recommended before sleeping to recite, "*Qul huwa Allahu ahad*" three times, "*Qul a`oodhu bi rabbi 'l-falaq,*" and "*Qul a`oodhu bi rabbi 'n-naas*" both one time. "*Qul huwa Allahu ahad*" takes you out of *shirk* to a divine area in Allah's Treasure, *Surat al-Falaq* gives you refuge in Allah from sorcery and *Surat an-Naas* protects you from the evil of *jinn*, the one who whispers in the hearts of people from human beings and from *jinn*, the "*sharri 'l-wawwasi 'l-khannaas,*" and that is the worst of *shayaateen* from *jinn* and human beings! (We recite it) because bad eyes from human beings can affect you. If Shaytan is entering through Door X or Door Y, the eyes of people are against each other. Envy and jealousy reflect bad, negative energy to the one you are jealous or envious of. So what do you need to do?

As we mentioned in the eight preceding lectures, Sayyidina `Ali ؏ said:

وعن علي بن أبي طالب قال: علمني رسول الله إذا نزل بي كرب أن أقول: لا إله إلا الله الحليم الكريم سبحان الله وتبارك الله رب العرش العظيم والحمد و رب العالمين.

Idhaa nazala bee karban an aqool laa ilaaha illa-Llah al-Haleem, al-Kareem, subhaan-Allahi, wa tabaarakallahu, Rabbu'l-`Arshi 'l-`Azheem, w' alhamdulillahi Rabbi 'l-`Alameen.

When an affliction came down or I was put in a difficulty, Prophet ﷺ taught me to say, "Laa ilaaha illa-Llah al-Haleem al-Kareem subhaan-Allahi wa tabaarakallahu Rabbu'l-`Arshi 'l-`Azheem, w'alhamdulillahi Rabbi 'l-`Alameen." (Musnad Ahmad, Nisa'ee and al-Haakim)

Reciting that will throw away a bad happening. Are we reading that *du`a*? No! This *du`a* prevents affliction from entering through a particular door. How many doors are there in the human body and how many are we going to close? There are three trillion doors in the body, a door on every cell in the body! If one cell is hurting the whole body hurts, as mentioned by the Prophet ﷺ that if a part of the body is hurting, the whole body will ache. So how can we close these doors? Allah is soft and patient with us; He will accept your repentance. Why do we remember Allah ﷻ when we are ill? We do not remember Him all our lives, but when we get sick we remember Him and say, "*Yaa Allah, yaa Hayyu, yaa Qayyum!*" As the Prophet ﷺ used to raise his hands to Heaven and recite when something difficult would come on the *ummah*, "*Yaa Allah, yaa Hayyu, yaa Qayyum, yaa Allah bi-rahmatika nastagheeth.*"

Ibn Mas`ud ؓ said, "Anyone of the prophets who felt an affliction coming was able to take it away by reciting *tasbeeh*." You may recite any *tasbeeh* that comes to your heart from Allah's Beautiful Names and Attributes.

From Sayyidina al-Hasan, Du`a of the Sahaabi

It is related by Sayyidina al-Hasan ؓ, grandson of the Prophet ﷺ, from Ibn Abi ad-Dunya ؓ in his book *Kitab al-Mujabeen, Book of Those Whose Du`as Allah Accepted*:

> There was a Sahaabi ؓ from the *Ansar* in the time of the Prophet ﷺ who was a merchant who made good money. He traveled a lot and people invested their money with him and he brought good profit. One day he was traveling with some money and a thief stopped him. It was difficult to see his face as it was covered, and as he drew out his sword he said, "Put out all the money you have and on top of that, I am going to kill you, I will not leave you!" The Sahaabi ؓ said, "Take the money. What do you need from my blood?" The thief answered, "I am taking your money and I will also kill you." The Sahaabi ؓ said, "If you don't want to leave me alone, give me permission to pray four *raka`ats* before I die." "Pray as much as you like," said the thief, "I will kill you right here but if you want time to pray, I will give it to you." So that Sahaabi ؓ made *wudu*, prayed four *raka`ats* and then in the last *sajda* recited this *du`a*:

يَا وَدُودُ ، يَا ذَا الْعَرْشِ الْمَجِيدِ ، يَا فَعَّالُ لِمَا تُرِيدُ ، أَسْأَلُكَ بِعِزِّكَ الَّذِي لَا يُرَامُ ، وَمُلْكِكَ الَّذِي لَا يُضَامُ ، وَبِنُورِكَ الَّذِي مَلَأَ أَرْكَانَ عَرْشِكَ ، أَنْ تَكْفِيَنِي شَرَّ هَذَا اللِّصِّ ، يَا مُغِيثُ أَغِثْنِي ، يَا مُغِيثُ أَغِثْنِي ، يَا مُغِيثُ أَغِثْنِي

Yaa Wadood, yaa Wadood! Yaa Dhal-`Arshi 'l-Majeed! Yaa fa`aalan limaa tureed! As'aluka bi `izzika 'Lladhee laa yuraam wa bi-mulkika 'Lladhee laa yudaam wa bi-noorika 'Lladhee mala'a arkaana `arshika an takfiyanee sharra haadha 'Llis. Yaa Mugheethu, aghithnee! Yaa Mugheethu, aghithnee! Yaa Mugheethu, aghithnee!

O Loving One! O Lord of the Glorified Throne! O You Who does what He wants! I ask You through Your Might which cannot be harmed, and Your Dominion which can not be defeated, and Your Light which filled the pillars of Your Thrown, that You protect me from the evil of this thief! O Savior from Calamity, save me! O Savior from Calamity, save me! O Savior from Calamity, save me!

As soon as he finished his *du`a,* a knight began to approach with a *harbah,* big spear in his hand. He had it placed on the ears of his horse. When the thief looked at him, he approached him to fight. The knight killed the thief with just one strike. Then he came to the Companion of the Prophet ﷺ and said, "Stand up." The Sahaabi ؓ said, "For the sake of Allah ﷻ and Prophet ﷺ, may Allah give you my life! Who are you? Allah has saved me today by your hands!" He said, "I am an angel from the angels of the Fourth Heaven. When you made that *du`a,* after the first part I heard the doors of heavens cracking with a loud noise, *sam`itu bi abwaabi sama ar-rabi`a qaaqaa.* Then after the second part of your *du`a, dajja kabeera,* was making lots of noises. Then after the third part of your *du`a,* a voice came to me saying, 'Go and help that person!' I asked Allah to give me permission to kill him."

And Sayyidna al-Hasan ؓ (the narrator) said, "Whoever makes *wudu,* prays four *raka`ats* and makes this *du`a,* Allah will accept it from him regardless if that person has any afflictions or not."

But who doesn't have afflictions? If you have a nice life, you still may have too many sins. Whether you have a problem or not, if you make that *du`a* Allah ﷻ will shut that door of sickness. So it means we have to learn different *du`a*s as every *du`a* is like a doctor. When he examines you he says, "You are sick, take these tablets." He prescribes medicine that will cure that specific illness. A patient with diabetes must take the medicine for diabetes, otherwise they will not be cured. We believe that every *du`a* has an effect and a cure, but if we don't know any *du`as,* through our hearts with Allah's Beautiful Names and Attributes, Allah will accept.

And we mentioned that for a *du`a* to be accepted, you must bring a *sadaqa* in front of (to precede) your *du`a.* You have to give before or after the *du`a,* as Allah ﷻ said to the Prophet ﷺ:

خُذْ مِنْ أَمْوَالِهِمْ صَدَقَةً تُطَهِّرُهُمْ وَتُزَكِّيهِم بِهَا وَصَلِّ عَلَيْهِمْ إِنَّ صَلَاتَكَ سَكَنٌ لَّهُمْ وَاللَّهُ سَمِيعٌ عَلِيمٌ

Khudh min amwaalihim sadaqatan tutahhiruhum wa tuzakkeehim bihaa wa salli `alayhim inna salaataka sakanun lahum w'Allahu samee`un `aleem.

Take alms of their wealth, from which you may purify them and make them grow, and pray for them. Verily, your prayer is an assuagement for them. Allah is Hearer, Knower. *(Surat at-Tawbah, 9:103)*

Why do you pay the doctor when you visit him? He charges you before you leave; Allah likes you to give *sadaqa* in His Way. Give one euro, one pound, or one dollar in the box in your *masjid* or slaughter something and give to orphans or poor people. Give blankets or Holy Qur'an to people who cannot afford it. You have to give something that you will be cured through it. *Shukran li hasaanatihi...* Allah makes your *du`a* accepted, thanking you for the *sadaqa* you have given. We have to thank Allah, but He is so generous and merciful with us, saying, "O My servant! You made *du`a* and on top of that you gave *sadaqa*. I am going to give you, bless you, thank you, and raise you higher."

Also, sometimes you make *du`a* at a special time and Allah accepts it, such as one hour before *Fajr*, and we previously mentioned six special times in which *du`a* is accepted; you may go back and review them. That is why it is said, *ad-du`a silah al-m'umin*, "The *du`a* is the weapon of the believer." So our weapon is not a sword or a knife, a gun or a stone, our weapon is *du`a*!

Prophet ﷺ said:

من رأى منكم منكرا فليغيره بيده ، فإن لم يستطع فبلسانه ، فإن لم يستطع فبقلبه ، وذلك أضعف الإيمان . رواه مسلم

Man ra'a minkum munkaran fa 'l-yughayirahu bi yadihi fa man lam yast`ati fa bi lisaanihi fa in lam yast`ati fa bi qalbihi wa dhaalika ada`f al-imaan.

Whoever sees something wrong should try to change it with his hand and if he cannot, then with his tongue and if he cannot, then with his heart and that is the weakest level of faith. *(Muslim)*

"By hand" would be to write something to someone (such as an apology) and try to change it. If you cannot, then change it with your tongue by speaking and if not with your tongue, then by your heart through *du`a*, and that is the weakest of imaan. Without making *du`a*, you will not be safe and your sickness will not go away, especially spiritual sickness.

May Allah ﷻ forgive us and may Allah ﷻ bless us.

Wa min Allahi 't-tawfiq, bi ḥurmati 'l-ḥabīb, bi ḥurmati 'l-Fātiḥah.

And with Allah is success. For the sake of the Beloved, for his sake we recite the opening chapter of Holy Qur'an.

Supplicate in Places Where it is Accepted

Aʿūdhu billāhi min ash-Shayṭāni 'r-rajīm. Bismillāhi' r-Raḥmāni 'r-Raḥīm.
Nawaytu 'l-arbāʿīn, nawaytu 'l-ʿitikāf, nawaytu'l-khalwah, nawaytu 'l-ʿuzlah,
nawaytu 'r-riyāḍa, nawaytu 's-sulūk, lillāhi Taʿalā fī hādhā 'l-masjid.
Atīʿūllāha wa atīʿū 'r-Rasūla wa ūlī 'l-amri minkum.
Obey Allah, obey the Prophet, and obey those in authority among you. (4:59)

Dastūr, madad yā Sulṭān al-Awlīyā, Mawlana Shaykh Nazim al-Haqqani ق.
Dastūr, madad yā Sulṭān al-Awlīyā, Mawlana Shaykh ʿAbdAllah ad-Daghestani ق.

Allahumma salli `alaa Sayyidina Muhammad.* Now since I came back we began this series, "Shifaa' through Holy Qur'an." We sat eight times already to talk about the importance of the Holy Qur'an in our life and we explained the effect of *du`a through the Holy Qur'an, that it will have more effect on human beings than normal medicine if they believe in what they are reading.

Many people, all of us, not necessarily all but many, many people buy a lot of books, all kinds of books, and for all the books people read they pay money to get it and when you read it, what do you do with it? You put it aside as it is finished. And authors, what did they do? They cheated you by taking your money and giving you a book of their invention which is not real! The only book you get wealth and benefit from is not authored by human beings, but it is the Holy Qur'an that Allah ﷻ has sent to human beings as a mercy:

وَنُنَزِّلُ مِنَ الْقُرْآنِ مَا هُوَ شِفَاء وَرَحْمَةٌ لِّلْمُؤْمِنِينَ وَلاَ يَزِيدُ الظَّالِمِينَ إَلاَّ خَسَارًا

Wa nunazzilu mina al-qur'ani ma huwa shifaa'un wa rahmatun li 'l-mu'mineen wa laa yazeedu 'zh-zhaalimeen illa khasaara.

And We sent down in the Qur'an such things that have healing and mercy for the believers and those who are oppressors to themselves.

(Surat al-'Israa, 17:82)

"*Wa laa yazeedu 'zh-zhaalimeen illa khasaara,*" and those who are oppressors to themselves by not reading the Holy Qur'an are the losers! So it means what Allah ﷻ has put of His Secrets in the Holy Qur'an, because it is the Words of Allah ﷻ, every word in the Holy Qur'an is divine, not created; it belongs to the Creator. The Holy Qur'an is not created, it is Allah's Words and when you say, *"Yaa Rahman, yaa Wadood, yaa Allah,"* it is divine. All His Beautiful Names and Attributes and all the words in the Holy Qur'an—any word, even *qul,* "say!"— is it not from Holy Qur'an? If you mean to say *"qul,"* that is from Holy Qur'an then it is divine. Outside the Holy Qur'an, nothing is divine. If we say "Alif," is it divine? Yes, it is *"Alif. Laam. Meem."* and therefore, it is divine.

Any divine word carries with it cure. As we said this morning, there are two kinds of diseases, physical and spiritual. Which is more difficult (to treat) than the other? The spiritual is more difficult because you don't pay attention to it and it is molded with your self, your ego with your soul, and you cannot throw it away. It is very difficult. Physical illnesses sometimes come and doctors try their best to cure you by some prescription, but what they prescribe always has side effects and is not going to be 100% clean. But if they prescribed a verse of Holy Qur'an to you as your cure that is 100% clean.

If you have real belief in Allah and His Prophet ﷺ, for sure when you read that verse you will be cured, but you need the guide, the one who knows which verse cures your sickness. Like we said today, you go to the pharmacy and you see hundreds and hundreds of medicines and if the doctor doesn't give you the right medicine, either you get nothing out of it or you get side effects. But the Holy Qur'an has no side effects; it is cured completely!

This morning we discussed why people get different sicknesses, because there are different doors in the body that Shaytan can come in. Every cell of the human beings is a door through which Shaytan comes in and you get affected by the sickness that Shaytan is carrying with it. You come to Y door, A door, B door, C door, and every door has a Shaytan that can enter through it and spray you with its dirtiness and the body will get different sickness.

So how should you get rid of sickness? What do you do? You go to the doctor to take medicine, but that doesn't close the door; Shaytan can still come, perhaps a smaller Shaytan. You feel you are getting cured, that the sickness is less and less, but that is temporary. You might get another sickness, Allah knows the hearts, but if you get a verse of Holy Qur'an that door will be closed completely. The *awliyaullah* have closed all the doors in themselves through which Shaytan can come, which is how they know verses to use to cure you completely and close those doors.

Du`a of the Sahaabi Saved from Murder

There was a Companion of the Prophet ﷺ who was a businessman who bought and sold, and people invested money with him as he was a pious, sincere servant of Allah ﷻ.

One day on a trip, a thief saw him, followed him and said, "Give me everything you have and I am going to kill you!" That poor Sahaabi ؓ looked at him and said, *"La hawla wa laa quwwata illa billah*! How I came on this problem? Okay, I'll give you the money, but let me free, why do you need my blood?"

The thief said, "No, this money is mine and whether you like it or not, I will take your money and then kill you!" Like today they take your money and then kill you so you cannot be witness against them, but where are you going to hide from Allah? May Allah forgive us!

The Sahaabi ؓ said, "If you are going to kill me, let my last moments be in Allah's Hands, let me make *wudu* and pray four *raka`ats*."

The thief said, "Who cares? Pray as much as you like. I am here and going to take your money and then kill you!"

So the man prayed four *raka`ats* and in his *sajda*, he said:

يَا وَدُودُ ، يَا وَدُودُ ، يَا ذَا الْعَرْشِ الْمَجِيدِ ، يَا فَعَّالُ لِمَا تُرِيدُ ، أَسْأَلُكَ بِعِزّكَ الَّذِي لَا يُرَامُ ، وَمُلْكِكَ الَّذِي لَا يُضَامُ ، وَبِنُورِكَ الَّذِي مَلَأَ أَرْكَانَ عَرْشِكَ ، أَنْ تَكْفِيَنِي شَرَّ هَذَا اللِّصِّ ، يَا مُغِيثُ أَغِثْنِي ، يَا مُغِيثُ أَغِثْنِي ، يَا مُغِيثُ أَغِثْنِي

Yaa Wadood, yaa Wadood! Yaa Dhal-`Arshi 'l-Majeed! Yaa fa`aalan limaa tureed! As'aluka bi `izzika 'Lladhee laa yuraam wa bi-mulkika 'Lladhee laa yudaam wa bi-noorika 'Lladhee mala'a arkaana `arshika an takfiyanee sharra haadha 'Llis. Yaa Mugheethu, aghithnee! Yaa Mugheethu, aghithnee! Yaa Mugheethu, aghithnee!

O Loving One! O Lord of the Glorified Throne! O You Who does what He wants! I ask You through Your Might which can not be harmed, and Your Dominion which can not be defeated, and Your Light which filled the pillars of Your Thrown, that You protect me from the evil of this thief! O Savior of Calamity, save me! O Savior of Calamity, save me! O Savior of Calamity, save me!

As soon as he finished a *faris* approached, a knight on a horse with a big spear that rested across its ears, and the burglar saw him coming. That *faris* came to him and killed him without asking any question, then he said to the Companion ؓ of the Prophet ﷺ, "Stand up."

The Companion ؓ said, "For Allah's sake, who are you?"

He said:

أَنَا مَلَكٌ مِنَ السَّمَاءِ الرَّابِعَةِ ، دَعَوْتَ اللَّهَ بِدُعَائِكَ الْأَوَّلَ ، فَسَمِعْتُ لِأَبْوَابِ السَّمَاءِ قَعْقَعَةً ، ثُمَّ دَعَوْتَ بِدُعَائِكَ الثَّانِي ، فَسَمِعْتُ لِأَهْلِ السَّمَاءِ ضَجَّةً ، ثُمَّ دَعَوْتَ بِدُعَائِكَ الثَّالِثِ ، فَقِيلَ لِي : دُعَاءُ مَكْرُوبٍ ، فَسَأَلْتُ اللَّهَ تَعَالَى أَنْ يُولِيَنِي قَتْلَهُ

I am an angel from Heaven, from the Fourth Paradise. When you prayed and supplicated the first du`a, the Doors of Heaven began to hear cracking, then you made du`a with the second part and the People of Heavens began to hear commotion, then you made the third du`a and a voice came to me, saying, "This person making du`a is in need of someone," and so I came to you asking Allah ﷻ to send me to kill that burglar.

That is why al-Hasan ؓ, the grandson of the Prophet ﷺ, mentioned that Hadith and also said:

مَنْ تَوَضَّأَ ، وَصَلَّى أَرْبَعَ رَكَعَاتٍ ، وَدَعَا بِهَذَا الدُّعَاءِ ، اسْتُجِيبَ لَهُ ، مَكْرُوبٌ كَانَ ، أَوْ غَيْرُ مَكْرُوبٍ

Whoever makes wudu and prays four raka`ats and makes this du`a, Allah will answer him if he has a problem or not and he will get what he wants.

Who do we believe? Allah! Look, he called on Allah in Allah's Beautiful Names and Attributes and Allah answered! So why aren't we answered when we make *du`a*, someone might ask this question. Because it has rules and principles. If you don't follow the rules and principles, we cannot say that your *du`a* will not be accepted as all *du`a*s are accepted, but the answer will be delayed.

Once in Ramadan, when the Sahaabah ؓ prayed *taraweeh* behind the Prophet ﷺ and Jibreel ؑ came down with Divine Revelation and he could not come down all the way, the Prophet ﷺ said, "Yaa Jibreel, come down," and Jibreel ؑ said, "I cannot and the other angels cannot come down further." Prophet ﷺ said, "Why?" Jibreel ﷺ said, "Because there is a smell and we are subtle beings and we cannot carry that smell, we are coming from Heavens." Prophet said, "What is that smell?" and Jibreel said, "Onions and garlic."

Grandshaykh ق said, "There are seventy illnesses that doctors cannot cure which can be cured by onions and garlic." So some of the Sahaabah ؓ had eaten onions and garlic that night and the angels could not descend with the revelation, so the Prophet ﷺ ordered those Sahaabah ؓ who had eaten onions and garlic to leave so that the manifestation could down. The smell of garlic and onions on your breath prevents angels from reaching you, and angels are the ones that take the *du`a*, that take the prayer, that take your good *`amal*, if they cannot approach you and reach you, what will happen? That *du`a* is delayed.

So the Prophet ﷺ said, "Let the Sahaabah who ate onions and garlic move back and pray separately and whatever rewards we receive from Allah we will share with you."

A Sahaabi ؓ will never leave Prophet ﷺ; they didn't move and Prophet ﷺ knew why they didn't move, so he sent Sayyidina `Umar ؓ, saying, "*Yaa* `Umar, pass by every Sahaabi ؓ and smell their breath to see which ones ate onions and garlic, then move them out," because he was waiting for the *tajalli* of that revelation to come. Immediately they knew they could not play with Sayyidina `Umar ؓ so they moved and Sayyidina Jibreel ؑ came down. So for *du`as* you must have a clean mouth, is it not?

That's why Allah ﷻ said:

فَإِذَا قَرَأْتَ الْقُرْآنَ فَاسْتَعِذْ بِاللَّهِ مِنَ الشَّيْطَانِ الرَّجِيمِ إِنَّهُ لَيْسَ لَهُ سُلْطَانٌ عَلَى الَّذِينَ آمَنُوا وَعَلَى رَبِّهِمْ يَتَوَكَّلُونَ

Fa idhaa qaraat al-Qur'an fasta`idh billahi min ash-Shaytani 'r-rajeem. Innahu laysa lahu sultaanun `alaa alladheena amanoo wa `alaa rabbihim yatawakaloon.

Now whenever you read this Qur'an, seek refuge with Allah from Shaytan, the Accursed. Behold, he has no power over those who have attained faith and who in their Sustainer place their trust. (Surat an-Nahl, 16:98-9)

It is very clear that *Ayatu sh-Shifaa`* are from the Qur'an and Allah is saying if you want to read Qur'an you have to seek refuge in Allah ﷻ from *Shaytani 'r-rajeem*, then he cannot approach you and since you sought refuge from Shaytan your *du`a* is clean, coming with cleanliness, and it will be taken up and accepted. Do we say, "*A`oodhu billahi min ash-Shaytani 'r-rajeem. Bismillahi 'r-Rahmani 'r-Raheem, alhamdulillahi rabbi 'l-`alameen was-*

salaatu was-salaam `alaa ashrafi 'l-mursaleen." So look, first recite "I seek refuge in Allah from *Shaytani 'r-rajeem,"* that is first. Then begin with *"Bismillahi 'r-Rahmani 'r-Raheem,"* as the Prophet ﷺ said:

كل عمل لم يبدأ باسم الله فهو أبتر

> *Any `amal which doesn't begin with Allah's Name is cut off, it has no continuity."*

So first we get rid of *Shaytani 'r-rajeem*, second we enter our new *`amal*, our *du`a*, with *Bismillahi 'r-Rahmani 'r-Raheem*. As soon as we say, *"Bismillahi 'r-Rahmani 'r-Raheem"* we say *"alhamdulillah*i rabbi 'l-`alameen," praising Allah and thanking Him. Then we wrap it, in order to be accepted with salawaat on the Prophet ﷺ, by reciting, *"Alhamdulillahi rabbi 'l-`alameen was-salaatu was-salaamu `alaa ashrafi 'l-mursaleen Sayyidina Muhammadin wa `alaa aalihi wa sahbihi ajma`een,"* and then begin with *du`a*.

Every *wali* from whom you ask *du`a,* in every moment there is a new manifestation to that area or place. The *du`a* here is different from *du`a* there. Every area has its own manifestation and effectiveness that changes from one place to another. It has different effects on different *du`a* that sometimes comes quickly and sometimes it does not, it depends on the area. If you pass by a movie theatre and make *du`a* there, maybe they make more money! Or if you pass by a restaurant that has all kinds of alcohol and you make *du`a* there, what will happen? But if you are in a *masjid* making *du`a,* is there a difference or not? There are holy places which are far better for making *du`a*:

كُلَّمَا دَخَلَ عَلَيْهَا زَكَرِيَّا الْمِحْرَابَ وَجَدَ عِندَهَا رِزْقاً قَالَ يَا مَرْيَمُ أَنَّى لَكِ هَـذَا قَالَتْ هُوَ مِنْ عِندِ اللّهِ إنَّ اللّهَ يَرْزُقُ مَن يَشَاء بِغَيْرِ حِسَابٍ

> *Whenever he (Zakariyya) entered her prayer niche, he found with her provision. He said, "O Mary! From where does this come to you?" She said, "From Allah, for Allah provides sustenance to whom He pleases without measure."* *(Surat Aali-`Imraan, 3:37)*

It is clear that every time Zakariyya ﷺ entered the niche of Maryam ﷺ he found sustenance there. Why? Because of her *du`a* and purity, Allah was sending physical and spiritual sustenance from Heavens to her and her place became holy. So Sayyidina Zakariyya ﷺ was ninety-nine years old and had no children. How many *du`as* he made, always asking to have a child!

Ninety-nine years and not given a child, until he entered the niche of Sayyida Maryam, where his *du`a* was accepted! He knew it had become a holy place. That is why *`ulama* say that *awliyaullah*'s places, as Sayyida Maryam is not a prophet, but she is a *waliya*, so her place became a holy place from too much *tajalli*, manifestation of Allah's Light and Allah's Beautiful Names and Attributes on that place and on her. So Sayyidina Zakariyya noticed that wisdom and went back to her private room and made *du`a* there, asking Allah for a child, although he said:

قَالَ رَبِّ إِنِّي وَهَنَ الْعَظْمُ مِنِّي وَاشْتَعَلَ الرَّأْسُ شَيْبًا وَلَمْ أَكُن بِدُعَائِكَ رَبِّ شَقِيًّا

He prayed, "O my Sustainer! Feeble have become my bones and my head glistens with grey hair, but never yet, O my Lord, has my prayer to You remained unanswered. (Surah Maryam, 19:4)

"My bones are becoming weak, *yaa Rabbee*, and my hair became white, but still I am asking for a child," at ninety-nine years old how do you get a child? Allah gave him Sayyidina Yahya because Jibreel came to him and showed him a miracle. So it depends where you make *du`a*.

In *Madinat al-Munawwara*, in front of the Prophet we are making *du`a*! *Tayyib*. Then why is it not accepted? It is the best place, or in front of *Ka`bah* we make *du`a*. Many get accepted and in reality all of them are accepted, as Allah's Last Name is as-Saboor: we do all kinds of sins and He is patient on us, as He said:

ادْعُونِي أَسْتَجِبْ لَكُمْ

Id`oonee astajib lakum.

Supplicate to Me and I will give you! (Surat al-Mu'min, 40:60)

But because of too many sins, Allah is keeping those *du`a* for us in the grave so that our grave does not become *hufrun min hufurun in-niraan*, a ditch from Hellfire! With these *du`as* Allah changes it to a piece of Paradise. So what do you want, *dunya* or *Akhirah*? We make *du`a* and we ask for acceptance. Sometimes it's like a perfect moon and you see the acceptance coming immediately, but other times it is delayed; nevertheless, keep asking, don't stop as we said before, that is the principle of *al-ilhaa*, to be persistent. You can go back on Sufilive.com to review this principle that we discussed earlier in this series. Allah wants us to be persistent in asking and asking and asking, non-stop! Allah will accept, Allah will cure you and Allah will forgive you!

I will give one example that I don't like to mention it many times, but for people to know. One time I was in New Jersey. Sometimes it happens and sometimes it does not. A *mureed* brought to me a lady from Ivory Coast who has two kids. Her husband was divorcing her and she began to have headaches. She went to a doctor and he said, "Do an MRI immediately" (for money) and he did it and said, "There is a tumor, cancer." They said it was a big tumor and that she would not live more than 3-4 months. She didn't say where in the head the tumor was. May Allah protect us from these kinds of sicknesses, so that we only go to see doctors for friendship and to drink coffee with them, not to examine us! Ameen! And she came carrying her two very young children and (the *mureed*) said, "Can you pray for her?" What to do?

I said, "*Inshaa-Allah,*" and we prayed for her and read *Surat al-Fatihah,* as the Prophet ﷺ said:

الفَاتِحَةُ لِمَا قُرِئَتْ لَهُ

Al-Fatihatu limaa quriyat lah.

The Fatihah is for whatever it is read.

So you read it for anything and Allah will accept. So I read the *Fatihah,* that's it; I didn't go through this or that *du`a.* Allah's *Fatihat al-Qur'an* is ... the Holy Qur'an carries the secrets of *az-Zaboor, Tawraat* and *Injeel;* secrets of the three other holy books are in the Holy Qur'an, and the heart of the Holy Qur'an is *Surat al-Yaseen* and the heart of *Yaseen* is *Surat al-Fatihah,* so from everything the secret is in these seven verses! I read that and then read on a bottle of water and gave it her. She said, "They want to do another MRI in a week." She took the bottle of water and after a week or sometime more, that *mureed* brought her to me again and she said to me, "They did the second MRI and no more tumor!" So she was cured. She is still living in New York. What happened? She had been cured by *Fatihah.* She was crying, that means she has very strong belief in her and when you have belief in Allah's Words you will be cured, but when you don't have belief in Allah's Words you will not be cured. You must have belief in Allah, in Holy Qur`an, in Holy Hadith of Prophet ﷺ and in the good *`amal* of *awliyaullah,* then you will be cured.

One day I was in my office and two or three people came to me from Texas and I saw them and said to myself, "I know this man and his wife." He didn't have children for 17 years. They came to me three years ago and said, "We've had no children for 17 years. Can you make *du`a*?" With our Mawlana Shaykh's *barakah*, I read *Surat al-Fatihah* on the lady with my stick and they went. Then after one year, I saw the man in the corridor and I called him. He said, "One second," and brought his wife carrying a baby, and they said, "This is the *Fatihah* baby."

And I give you another example. There is one man in London married for ten years, and I know him very well. He said, "We have no children."

I said, "*Inshaa-Allah* Allah will give you a child next year when we see you."

So in my pocket I had a KitKat chocolate bar and I read *Surat al-Fatihah* on it and said, "You eat half, let your wife eat half and *Inshaa-Allah* you will have a child." I came the next year but there was no child and I didn't say anything, I kept quiet, then the year after I went and his wife had a child! He said, "*Yaa* Shaykh! When you left and one year had passed, I didn't remember you gave me the chocolate; it was in the drawer! So when we were cleaning I found the KitKat and broke it in half. We each ate half and then we had a child." So without mentioning his name, they call him the "KitKat Child" and they are in North England.

So you don't know. And what Allah wants from you is to be clean! So this business man who was about to be killed asked to pray four *raka`ats*, and he made *wudu* and prayed, so you see *du`a* cannot be without *wudu* and it cannot be without prayer, and also it cannot be done without giving *sadaqa*.

خُذْ مِنْ أَمْوَالِهِمْ صَدَقَةً تُطَهِّرُهُمْ وَتُزَكِّيهِم بِهَا وَصَلِّ عَلَيْهِمْ إِنَّ صَلَاتَكَ سَكَنٌ لَهُمْ وَاللهُ سَمِيعٌ عَلِيمٌ

Khudh min amwaalihim sadaqatan tutahhiruhum wa tuzakkeehim bihaa wa salli `alayhim inna salaataka sakanun lahum w'Allahu samee`un `aleem.

Take alms of their wealth from which you may purify them and make them grow, and pray for them. Verily, your prayer is an assuagement for them. Allah is The Hearer, The Knower. (Surat at-Tawbah, 9:103)

Ibn Qayim said that many make *du`a* and it is accepted because either he did something that Allah is happy with or he gave a *sadaqa*, *hasanaat*, he helped someone for Allah to accept his *du`a*. So don't make *du`a* without spending or first doing a good deed. He gave something as a *sadaqa* (charity) before he came to pray the *du`a* and Allah granted him acceptance as a thank you for that charity.

Now too many people pray *du`a* and don't give charity. They are stingy and Allah is The Generous! You have to show Him generosity, not stinginess. Today we ask *du`a*, but don't give anything. No, give charity to a school, a *masjid*, a hospital, to someone who is teaching you and then present it to someone to make *du`a* for you or you make *du`a* as Allah ordered Prophet ﷺ in Holy Qur'an, "Take from them their wealth, clean them with it and purify them and then pray for them."

So how many steps?

1. Take from them;
2. Clean them with the charity;
3. Purify them; and,
4. When they are purified, pray for them because your prayer for them gives them *sakeenah*, tranquility. It means they will be cured.

May Allah give us cure by Holy Qur'an! Don't keep Holy Qur'an on the shelf, keep it in your heart and read even one page or a half page daily. If you don't know how to read, then open it and look because there is Light coming out of the verses of Holy Qur'an. It is not dead, it is divine, which means it is living forever! Allah's Words live forever and the Holy Qur'an is the only book living forever in Paradise! The language of angels and the People of Paradise is the Holy Qur'an, not just Arabic. Allah will open for you secrets how to read. You think Arabic cannot be expanded?

O Muslims and everywhere around the world! Every book you read is a waste of time, energy and money! The only book that rewards and gives you back in *dunya* and *Akhirah* is the Holy Qur'an. No other book can give you what Holy Qur'an gives you! So our duty is to keep respecting the Holy Qur'an (Mawlana raises the Holy Qur'an above his head).

May Allah ﷻ forgive us and may Allah ﷻ bless us.

Wa min Allahi 't-tawfiq, bi ḥurmati 'l-ḥabīb, bi ḥurmati 'l-Fātiḥah.

And with Allah is success. For the sake of the Beloved, for his sake we recite the opening chapter of Holy Qur'an.

Reading Holy Qur'an is Salvation from Punishment and the Path to Mercy

A'ūdhu billāhi min ash-Shayṭāni 'r-rajīm. Bismillāhi' r-Raḥmāni 'r-Raḥīm.
Nawaytu 'l-arbā'īn, nawaytu 'l-'itikāf, nawaytu'l-khalwah, nawaytu 'l-'uzlah,
nawaytu 'r-riyāḍa, nawaytu 's-sulūk, lillāhi Ta'alā fī hādhā 'l-masjid.
Atī'ūllāha wa atī'ū 'r-Rasūla wa ūlī 'l-amri minkum.
Obey Allah, obey the Prophet, and obey those in authority among you. (4:59)

Dastūr, madad yā Sulṭān al-Awlīyā, Mawlana Shaykh Nazim al-Haqqani ق.
Dastūr, madad yā Sulṭān al-Awlīyā, Mawlana Shaykh 'AbdAllah ad-Daghestani ق.

We have been discussing the importance *du`a* and how in every moment in our lives we must ask for Allah's forgiveness. If you look from the beginning of the Holy Qur'an to the end, every *ayah* is to save us: in every *ayah*, Allah ﷻ mentioned what we are doing bad and it is followed by something which tells us how we can get out of the bad. It means we are doing sins and Allah ﷻ wants us to repent, showing *Ayat al-`Adhaab,* a verse of divine punishment, and then followed by *Ayat al-Rahmat,* a verse of divine mercy. I heard from Grandshaykh, may Allah ﷻ bless his soul, say that for every Ayat al-*`adhaab* that comes in the Holy Qur'an, it is immediately followed by Ayat al-*rahmat,* which means Allah is showing us, "This is your problem, so be careful and this is the way out of it," and telling us to repent in every moment in our life through the Holy Qur'an.

وَنُنَزِّلُ مِنَ الْقُرْآنِ مَا هُوَ شِفَاء وَرَحْمَةٌ لِّلْمُؤْمِنِينَ وَلاَ يَزِيدُ الظَّالِمِينَ إَلاَّ خَسَارًا

> *Wa nunazzilu mina al-qur'ani ma huwa shifaa'un wa rahmatun li 'l-mu'mineen wa laa yuzeedu 'zh-zhaalimeen illa khasaara.*
>
> *And We sent down in the Qur'an such things that have healing and mercy for the believers and those who are oppressors to themselves.*
>
> *(Surat al-'Israa, 17:82)*

So the Holy Qur'an is not only *Ayaat ash-Shifaa`* to cure us, it is also to save us from the biggest sickness, the biggest disease, the most frightening element that people, especially *mu'min* and Muslims, think about, which is *Jahannam*! *Jahannam*'s punishment is for Muslims and *mu'min*s who did sins and did not repent! It is Allah's Mercy that He gave us the Holy Qur'an and after every verse of *`adhaab* that shows you deserve *Jahannam,* He gave us an *ayah* of *rahmah.* So if you don't read Holy Qur'an you are stuck as it is the way out of punishment and the way into mercy!

I was going to speak on something else, but this is important to mention and it is frightening. I will not mention the very, very frightening Hadith, but the moderate ones, because if you really think about it you will be sitting in a corner crying continuously and repenting, all of us, and not do anything, only crying.

عن أبي سعيد الخدري رضي الله عنه قال: قال رسول صلى الله عليه وسلم: ((كيف أنعم وقد التقم صاحب القرن القرن، وحنى جبهته، وأصغى سمعه، ينتظر أن يؤمر أن ينفخ، فينفخ، قال المسلمون: فكيف نقول يا رسول الله؟ قال: قولوا: حسبنا الله ونعم الوكيل، توكلنا على الله ربنا)).

Anna an-Nabi ﷺ qaala: kayfa an`amu wa saahibu's-soori qad altaqamahu w'asgha sam`ahu wa hana jabhatahu yantazhiru mataa yu'mar. Faqaaloo: Yaa Rasoolullah wa maa taa'murnaa? Qaala: qooloo hasbuna'Llah wa ni`ama'l-wakeel, wa tawakalnaa `ala 'Llaahi rabbunaa.

Ibn `Abbas ؓ narrated that the Prophet ﷺ said:

How will I enjoy myself when the one who is holding the trumpet is already holding it to his mouth ready to blow on it [and when he blows it, that will mean everything is dead. How am I going to live happily and in peace when Israfeel ؑ, the one who holds the trumpet, and I do not know the moment that he will blow in it and everything is finished? It is either (our destiny) to Heaven or Hellfire. How am I going to live happily? What do we have to say to save ourselves?]

Is everyone not worried if Prophet ﷺ is worried for us? He is the most worried for his *ummah*; he does not care for himself, but only for his *ummah.* That is why Allah ﷻ gave him higher and higher (stations) because he put his *ummah* in front. If he is caring for his *ummah* that they might be punished, then why are we not caring and thinking?

And the Sahaabah ؓ asked, what should they say to be saved? *Qooloo hasbun Allah wa ni`ma' l-wakeel.* He ﷺ said, "Recite '*hasbun Allah wa ni`ma 'l-wakeel.*'" That is why we have a daily *wird* to recite one-hundred to one-thousand times "*Hasbun Allah wa ni`ma 'l-wakeel.*" He said, "Say, '*Hasbun Allaah wa ni`ma 'l-wakeel tawakalnaa `ala 'Llaahi rabbunaa,*'" which means, "*Yaa*

Rabbee! There is no way out of our sins except through trust in You, our Lord!"

The Prophet ﷺ is teaching the Sahaabah ؓ to say "*Hasbun Allah wa ni`ma 'l-wakeel,*" so what do we have to say? *Hasbun Allah wa ni`ma 'l-wakeel*! Is it dangerous (to leave it) or not? Yes, of course it is! Ibn `Umar ؓ said, as narrated by Imam Ahmad in his *Musnad*, and it is one of the major problems that we are falling into, all humanity, from children up to parents, as if you ask a child, "Who knows better, you or your parents?" He will say, "We know better." It is obvious.

Ibn `Umar ؓ said, "Whoever thinks of himself as a big shot doesn't accept for anyone to say a word to him. He is stubborn, and whatever he thinks he takes it as correct and does not accept *naseeha*."

Prophet ﷺ said:

الدين نصيحة

Ad-deenu naseeha.
Religion is advice.

Prophet ﷺ came to give you advice, yes, but he also came for more—to carry—but advice is religion. People don't care for advice today, they don't listen or they only want what their own mind tells them. That is why guides, *maashayikh*, are important in your life, although not everyone or every shaykh, and we will come through this later, about those who cheat people, the charlatans. I like what one big scholar said, although we don't agree with some of his teachings, but even he was giving them a right label or description when they asked him about the shaykhs in *tasawwuf*, because he was following Sayyidina `Abdul Qadir al-Jilani ق, a big scholar of his time whom, until today, too many people are following him. He said there are three different kinds of Sufi's:

Shaykhs of Tariqah That Keep Shari`ah

Those who are real guides, *al-mashayikh al-sufiyyah al-haqiqiyya*, the real ones who keep Shari`ah. They do not accept *tariqah* without Shari`ah as Shari`ah comes first and *tariqah* comes second. Never say *tariqah* comes first as it can never be! It's always Shari`ah first, then *tariqah*. These are the ones about whom Allah ﷻ mentioned in the Holy Qur'an:

أَلا إِنَّ أَوْلِيَاءَ اللَّهِ لاَ خَوْفٌ عَلَيْهِمْ وَلاَ هُمْ يَحْزَنُونَ

Alaa inna awliyaaullaahi laa khawfun `alayhim wa laa hum yahzanoon.

Behold! Verily on the Friends of Allah there is no fear, nor shall they grieve.

(Surah Yunus, 10:62)

These have been mentioned in the Hadith that he authenticated and mentioned in his book, *Majmu`a Fatawah Ibn Taymiyyah.*

من عادا لي وليا فقد آذنته بالحرب

Man `adaa lee waliyyan faqad aadhantahu bi 'l-harb.

(Allah [swt] said) Whoever comes against My wali, I declare war on him.

(Hadith Qudsi; Bukhari, from Abu Hurayrah)

That Hadith was authenticated by him and its roots were restored! And he also authenticated:

أولياء الله تحت قبابي لا يعلمهم غيري

Awliyaa'ee tahta qibaabee, laa ya`lamuhum ghayree.

My saints are under my domes; no one knows them except me.

(Hadith Qudsee)

Professional Shaykhs

Al-Muhtarifoon, "professionals," are those who have knowledge and make a business out of *tasawwuf*, not like making a mosque, school or hospital, but they pocket the money. And there are many shaykhs who receive a lot of money but their children take it; these are the professionals, *muhktarifoon.*

The Charlatans

The charlatans; he called them that because they have no knowledge and they guide people through imaginary knowledge. They don't observe the

Shari`ah, but they blend their *tasawwuf* with all kinds of beliefs and they are charlatans.

These are the three groups. The first group tries to save themselves by telling their egos, "You are not a big shot." Allah pulled them from *ta`zheem an-nafs* as He said in Holy Qur'an:

فَلَا تُزَكُّوا أَنفُسَكُمْ

Fa laa tuzakoo anfusakum.
Don't praise yourself. (Surat an-Najm, 53:32)

Those who are praising their egos are like us here, don't we praise our egos? We cannot accept anyone else's opinion except what we say. And that is why Ibn `Umar ؓ mentioned this `amal in the Hadith:

من تعظم في نفسه أو اختال في مشيته ، لقي الله عز وجل و هو عليه غضبان

Man ta`zhama fee nafsihi aw akhtaala fee mashiyyatihi laqiyy 'Llahu `azza wa jalla wa Huwa `alayhi ghadbaan.
Who thinks he is a big shot or when he walks is proud of himself like a peacock and there are bodyguards with him...

That is why Prophet ﷺ said it is *haraam* (to wear clothes that trail behind) because in the time of *jahiliyyah*, ignorance, they used to have longer dresses, garments that swept the floor when they walked, just like brides' dresses, to show that they were the leaders of the community and Prophet ﷺ prohibited that.

The Hadith continues:

He is going to be judged on the Day of Judgment and Allah ﷻ is going to be angry with him because kibr (pride) is only for Allah ﷻ.

And Allah ﷻ said, *al-kibru ridaaee*, "Arrogance is My garment, it's only for Me."

قال الله تعالى في حديث قدسي:" الكبر ردائي, و العظمة ازاري, فمن نازعني في واحد منهما, رميته في جهنم و لا ابالي

Pride is My upper garment and Greatness is my lower wrap. And whoever competes with me in My Greatness and in My Arrogance, I will throw him in Hellfire and I don't care. (Hadith Qudsee)

So then how are we making ourselves arrogant? We are proud and we teach our children to be proud and we pride ourselves for no reason. Such a person will be facing Allah ﷻ on the Day of Judgment and He will be angry with him. You know that Prophet ﷺ said, "Don't make your father angry," because the anger of the father brings the anger of Allah ﷻ on you, and that is for anger of a father, so what do you think about the anger of Allah ﷻ? Many people make their parents angry, is it not? Yes, and Allah ﷻ prohibited that.

Allah ﷻ says in Holy Qur'an:

وَقَضَى رَبُّكَ أَلاَّ تَعْبُدُواْ إِلاَّ إِيَّاهُ وَبِالْوَالِدَيْنِ إِحْسَانًا إِمَّا يَبْلُغَنَّ عِندَكَ الْكِبَرَ أَحَدُهُمَا أَوْ كِلاَهُمَا فَلاَ تَقُل لَّهُمَآ أُفٍّ وَلاَتَنْهَرْهُمَا وَقُل لَّهُمَا قَوْلاً كَرِيمً

Wa qadaa rabbuka alaa ta`budoo illa iyyaahu wa bi 'l-waalidayni ihsaanan, immaa yablughanna `indaka al-kibara ahaduhumaa aw kilaahumaa falaa taqu'l-lahumaa uffin wa laa tanharhumaa waqu'l-lahumaa qawlan kareema.

Allah has decreed not to worship anyone except Me and with your mother and father to be nice with them. Whether one or both of them attain old age in their life, say not to them a word of contempt, nor repel them, but address them in terms of honor. *(Surat al-'Israa, 17:23)*

Only say, *sam`ina wa a`tanaa,* "I am listening and accepting!" You are not allowed to even say *"uff"* even if they are non-Muslim. As long as they don't interfere in your religion you have to serve them; if they ask you to take them to the church to pray it's your duty to take them there and you should stand by the door and allow them to go in and pray, and when they come out you take them back home. This is Islam and we have to be very careful.

There might be people who don't pray as they are drunk so they don't care.

It is mentioned in the Hadith from `Abdullah Ibn `Amru in the *Musnad,* that Prophet ﷺ said:

عَنْ رَسُولِ اللَّهِ صَلَّى اللَّهُ عَلَيْهِ وَسَلَّمَ ، قَالَ : " مَنْ تَرَكَ الصَّلاةَ سُكْرًا مَرَّةً وَاحِدَةً ، فَكَأَنَّمَا كَانَتْ لَهُ الدُّنْيَا وَمَا عَلَيْهَا فَسُلِبَهَا ، وَمَنْ تَرَكَ الصَّلاةَ سُكْرًا أَرْبَعَ مَرَّاتٍ كَانَ حَقًّا عَلَى اللَّهِ أَنْ يَسْقِيَهُ مِنْ طِينَةِ الْخَبَالِ " ، قِيلَ : وَمَا طِينَةُ الْخَبَالِ ؟ قَالَ : " عُصَارَةُ أَهْلِ جَهَنَّمَ "

The Prophet ﷺ says, "Those who dropped their prayer because they were drunk (and you do not pray because it could be that you don't believe or you don't care or you are doing something unacceptable) it is equal in owning the whole wealth of this dunya and then he loses it in one shot."

That is for missing one of your daily prayers, so then think well about your prayers! Are we going to lose our prayers? And who is responsible for the children? He (*mureed*) knows the time of the prayer and he is a young child, but we (adults) don't know. He knows it by the minute. What time is *Zhuhr*? (12:39 p.m.). He is better than all of us. It means he is ready and when 12:39 p.m. comes, he is going to pray.

And the Hadith continues:

And anyone who leaves his prayer four times because he is drunk, Allah is going to give him the mud of Khubaal. And the Sahaabah *asked the Prophet ﷺ, "What is that mud of Khubaal?" He said, "It is the juice that comes when you compress Hellfire with all the people in it and you will be given that juice to drink."*

That is for leaving four prayers, so then ask yourself, are we leaving prayers or not? Leave asking others, think!

قال رسول الله صلى الله عليه وسلم : من شرب الخمر لم يقبل الله له صلاة أربعين صباحا ، فإن تاب تاب الله عليه ...

Prophet ﷺ also said:

Whoever drinks wine one time, Allah will reject his prayers for forty days even if he repents...

And for leaving one prayer you will get the juice of Hellfire! O People! We have to be very careful. What will save us? *Du`a*! Keep doing *du`a*! *"Hasbun Allah wa ni`mal wakeel ala 'l-laahi tawakalna ni`mal mawla wa ni`man naseer subhaanaka rabbana wa ilayka 'l-maseer."* There are many *du`as* that we have mentioned before.

If that person repents, Allah will not accept forty prayers from him as if he lost them, and if you lose one prayer as mentioned above, you are in a bad situation. However, if that person's repentance is real, Allah ﷻ will forgive him, but if he goes back to it, for sure his food is going to be the juice of Hellfire! We must not let ourselves fall into this; what happened has passed, but today we repent and those who are hearing us (on the Internet) should make repentance and we must not lose one prayer! We have to be careful. I am saying this to myself and to anyone who is hearing it. May Allah ﷻ forgive us.

Who are the best of people? Not those who have the strongest faith; those are from the last *ummah*, but the best people are the *anbiya*. And Ibn Qayyim warns in his book, *al-Jawaab al-Kafee*:

كما أن خير الناس الأنبياء ، فشر الناس من تشبه بهم يوهم أنه منهم وليس منهم، فخير الناس بعدهم العلماء والشهداء والصديقون والمخلصون، وشر الناس من تشبه بهم يوهم أنه منهم وليس منهم

The best people are the anbiya, and the worst people are those who appear like them and delude others that they are from them, but they are not from them. And the best of people after them [al-anbiya] are the scholars and the martyrs and the veracious ones and the sincere ones, and the worst of people are those who appear like them and delude others that they are from them, but they are not from them.

So the worst people are those who come and say, "We are part of them, we are like them." These are people who declare prophecy and they are liars. They are the worst of people! Who are the best people after *anbiya*? *Awliya, `ulama, shuhaada* and *siddiqeen*. After the best ones, the worst ones are those who *yoohim,* make it look like he is one of them but he is not, because people will listen to him after he makes them think he is one of them, as if he is a *wali* or *siddiq* or *shaheed* and people believe him. There are too many like them!

How many *tariqats* are there? Forty-one real ones, but out of these there are hundreds of thousands! There are many branches and everyone claims he is right and the others are wrong and if these branches are not following the footsteps of their *shuyookh,* the real guided ones, they are charlatans and misleading people. When you mislead people you are facing a big problem! May Allah ﷻ save us from that, because when they tell you something you believe that they will not lie to you, but they are lying to themselves because they might imagine they have connections, but that is Shaytan's connection, not *ar-Rahmaan's* connection. So they are like what Iblees said, "I am going to cheat them and make them fall to their own desires, thinking those desires are good."

Like Iblees came to Sayyidina Adam ﷺ and said:

يَا آدَمُ هَلْ أَدُلُّكَ عَلَى شَجَرَةِ الْخُلْدِ وَمُلْكٍ لَّا يَبْلَى

Yaa Adam hal aduluka `alaa shajarati 'l-khuldi wa mulkin laa yablaa.

O Adam! Shall I lead you to the Tree of Eternity and to a kingdom that never decays? *(Surah TaHa, 20:120)*

He told him it was the Tree of Eternity, and, "If you eat from it, all these kingdoms will be yours forever!" If he cheated Adam ﷺ, can he not cheat us? We have to be very careful. So what do we have to say? *Hasbun Allah wa ni`ma 'l-wakeel.* Today *"hasbun Allah wa ni`ma 'l-wakeel"* came through these *ahadith* and there are lots, but we cannot go through all of them. May Allah ﷻ forgive us!

I will mention one more. In *Sahih Muslim,* Sayyidina Abu Hurayrah ؓ said:

قَالَ تَفَرَّقَ النَّاسُ عَنْ أَبِي هُرَيْرَةَ فَقَالَ لَهُ قَائِلٌ مِنْ أَهْلِ الشَّامِ أَيُّهَا الشَّيْخُ حَدِّثْنِي حَدِيثًا سَمِعْتَهُ مِنْ رَسُولِ اللَّهِ صَلَّى اللَّهُ عَلَيْهِ وَسَلَّمَ قَالَ نَعَمْ سَمِعْتُ رَسُولَ اللَّهِ صَلَّى اللَّهُ عَلَيْهِ وَسَلَّمَ يَقُولُ أَوَّلُ النَّاسِ يُقْضَى لَهُمْ يَوْمَ الْقِيَامَةِ ثَلَاثَةٌ رَجُلٌ اسْتُشْهِدَ فَأُتِيَ بِهِ فَعَرَّفَهُ نِعَمَهُ فَعَرَفَهَا قَالَ فَمَا عَمِلْتَ فِيهَا قَالَ قَاتَلْتُ فِيكَ حَتَّى اسْتُشْهِدْتُ قَالَ كَذَبْتَ وَلَكِنَّكَ قَاتَلْتَ لِيُقَالَ فُلَانٌ جَرِيءٌ فَقَدْ قِيلَ ثُمَّ أُمِرَ بِهِ فَسُحِبَ عَلَى وَجْهِهِ حَتَّى أُلْقِيَ فِي النَّارِ وَرَجُلٌ تَعَلَّمَ الْعِلْمَ وَعَلَّمَهُ وَقَرَأَ الْقُرْآنَ فَأُتِيَ بِهِ فَعَرَّفَهُ نِعَمَهُ فَعَرَفَهَا قَالَ فَمَا عَمِلْتَ فِيهَا قَالَ تَعَلَّمْتُ الْعِلْمَ وَعَلَّمْتُهُ وَقَرَأْتُ فِيكَ الْقُرْآنَ قَالَ كَذَبْتَ وَلَكِنَّكَ تَعَلَّمْتَ الْعِلْمَ لِيُقَالَ عَالِمٌ وَقَرَأْتَ الْقُرْآنَ لِيُقَالَ قَارِئٌ فَقَدْ قِيلَ ثُمَّ أُمِرَ بِهِ فَسُحِبَ عَلَى وَجْهِهِ حَتَّى أُلْقِيَ فِي النَّارِ وَرَجُلٌ وَسَّعَ اللَّهُ عَلَيْهِ وَأَعْطَاهُ مِنْ أَصْنَافِ الْمَالِ كُلِّهِ فَأُتِيَ بِهِ فَعَرَّفَهُ نِعَمَهُ فَعَرَفَهَا فَقَالَ مَا عَمِلْتَ فِيهَا قَالَ مَا تَرَكْتُ مِنْ سَبِيلٍ تُحِبُّ قَالَ أَبُو عَبْد الرَّحْمَن وَلَمْ أَفْهَمْ تُحِبُّ كَمَا أَرَدْتُ أَنْ يُنْفَقَ فِيهَا إِلَّا أَنْفَقْتُ فِيهَا لَكَ قَالَ كَذَبْتَ وَلَكِنْ لِيُقَالَ إِنَّهُ جَوَادٌ فَقَدْ قِيلَ ثُمَّ أُمِرَ بِهِ فَسُحِبَ عَلَى وَجْهِهِ فَأُلْقِيَ فِي النَّارِ

I heard Prophet ﷺ saying "The first people that will be judged on the Day of Judgment are three groups or types of people: someone who died in the way of Allah, he is shaheed, a martyr. They bring him to judgment and show him ni`amullah, Allah's Favors. He knew a martyr will get these favors. (And) one of the angels will ask, 'What you have done to deserve these favors?' He will say to Allah ﷻ, 'I went to fight in Your way until I died.' (And this is very important for politicians to know about Islam about martyrdom, especially suicide bombing). He will be asked, these favors, what did you do to deserve them?' He will say, 'I fought for You, I went for jihad, holy war. Allah will say, 'Fa qaala kadhdhabta—you lie! (You went to fight, putting on your body *all kinds of bombs, killing yourself when I gave you a soul that is haraam to kill) and you killed yourself for people to say you are courageous.'*

And this is what is happening today. In order to say this they put a 'martyr' on TV, showing his picture and a banner saying, "He died in the way of Allah ﷻ." What is Allah saying in *Sahih Muslim*, narrated by Abu Hurayra? "You are a liar, you are not correct in what you are doing; you did it in order to make yourself *jareer* that you are 'daring' to go and fight! This is to raise your ego, it's not for Me! You killed these innocent people to show you are *jareer*, courageous!"

When Sayyidina `Ali wanted to fight that wrestler (who challenged him), the Prophet ﷺ did not permit him due to an illness in his eye. And that wrestler went on cursing Sayyidina `Ali, so then Prophet ﷺ permitted him to go ahead and he ﷺ read (a *du`a*) on his eye. Sayyidina `Ali confronted the wrestler, and the law in those days was to kill if you could put your enemy on the ground; he had to surrender. So Sayyidina `Ali overcame the wrestler and put him on the ground. The wrestler said:

"Kill me!" And he spat on his face.

Sayyidina `Ali dropped the sword and said, "I am not going to kill you, you can leave."

He asked, "Why? Kill me, I am the one that can take it, kill me!"

Sayyidina `Ali said, "If I kill you now, I am killing you for my ego because you spat on my face. My ego is angry, I cannot kill you for my ego that was only for (coming against) Allah ﷻ."

And the wrestler said, "If that is Islam, I am (now) a Muslim!" And he became a Muslim.

So those people who go to fight and to kill (in false holy wars), as it is mentioned in the above Hadith in *Sahih Muslim*, Allah ﷻ will call them on the Day of Judgment and say, "*Fa qaala kadhibta,* You are liars! You only killed for fame, that is not *jihad fee sabeelillah*, jihad in Allah's Way. You fought for people to say 'He is courageous,' and everyone said that, they didn't know your intentions, but I know it and you became famous, but now you will not get a title of being martyrs from Me, you are just normal people."

And their titles will be thrown in their faces, as Allah ﷻ said in Holy Qur'an:

وَقَدِمْنَا إِلَى مَا عَمِلُوا مِنْ عَمَلٍ فَجَعَلْنَاهُ هَبَاء مَّنثُورًا

Wa qadimnaa ilaa maa `amiloo min `amalin fa-ja`alnaahu habaa'an manthoora.

And We shall turn to whatever deeds they did (in this life), and We shall make such deeds as scattered dust. *(Surat al-Furqaan, 25:23)*

He will be judged as a normal person, not a martyr.

Prophet ﷺ continues the Hadith:

At that time umira bihi, Allah orders the angels to pull him and throw him on his face in the Hellfire.

That is for the one who is considered martyr in the eyes of people, but in Allah's Eyes he is lying. So what are we going to do? *Hasbun Allah wa ni`ma 'l-wakeel.*

The second group is when a man who learned Islamic knowledge and read the Holy Qur'an and became an *`alim*. Allah shows him His Favors and says, "What did you do to deserve these favors?" and he says, "I learned knowledge and Holy Qur'an and taught it," and Allah will say, "*Fa qaala* kadhibta, you are a liar! You studied so that people will praise you and say, 'O! He is a scholar.'"

And today there are too many like in the example before, the martyrs, and now *`ulama*; they give you a *fatwa* about suicide bombing. Did they not read this Hadith? Of course they read it! What are they going to answer? The Hadith continues:

And you read the Holy Qur'an in order for people to say, 'He is qaari, a hafizh.' Allah will order the angels to pull him away from His Presence and throw him on his face in Hellfire.

There are too many today who claim they are *hafizh* and *qaari*. It is good (to be that), but you must have discipline.

The third group is when someone whom Allah ﷻ gave richness, too much money (and there are too many today) and Allah shows His Favors and says, "What did you do to deserve these?" He says, "You gave me a lot of wealth and I spent that money in Your Way, I didn't keep it." Allah says,

"*Qaal kadhibt*, you are a liar! You did that for people to say, 'This man is a good man, generous in the Way of Allah,' in order for people to praise you, not praise Me; you were trying to get the attention to yourself!" And Allah will order the angels to pull him on his face and throw him in Hellfire. These are the first three groups that will make Hellfire to burn intensely because they are dumped in it.

May Allah forgive us. May Allah ﷻ bless us.

Do you know that when you read Hadith of Prophet ﷺ or you read a verse of the Holy Qur'an, that verse will talk because it is living; it will ask forgiveness on your behalf! Any Hadith you read like this, that causes fear, will take that sin and the sickness from you and it will dump them in Hellfire and you will become clean! May Allah make us clean for the sake of Sayyidina Muhammad ﷺ and for the sake of Holy Qur'an and Holy Hadith and *awliyaullah*!

May Allah ﷻ forgive us and may Allah ﷻ bless us.

Wa min Allahi 't-tawfiq, bi ḥurmati 'l-ḥabīb, bi ḥurmati 'l-Fātiḥah.

And with Allah is success. For the sake of the Beloved, for his sake we recite the opening chapter of Holy Qur'an.

Real Martyrdom

Aʿūdhu billāhi min ash-Shayṭāni 'r-rajīm. Bismillāhi' r-Raḥmāni 'r-Raḥīm.
Nawaytu 'l-arbāʿīn, nawaytu 'l-ʿitikāf, nawaytu'l-khalwah, nawaytu 'l-ʿuzlah,
nawaytu 'r-riyāḍa, nawaytu 's-sulūk, lillāhi Taʿalā fī hādhā 'l-masjid.
Atīʿūllāha wa atīʿū 'r-Rasūla wa ūlī 'l-amri minkum.
Obey Allah, obey the Prophet, and obey those in authority among you. (4:59)

Dastūr, madad yā Sulṭān al-Awlīyā, Mawlana Shaykh Nazim al-Haqqani ق.
Dastūr, madad yā Sulṭān al-Awlīyā, Mawlana Shaykh ʿAbdAllah ad-Daghestani ق.

I think you should laugh a little bit more before we begin, because after we begin I think you are going to cry, not really to cry, but we will explain more of *daa wa 'd-dawaa*, sickness and what cures it, and how to be cured, why we get sick, as we explained that the last two weeks in about ten lectures, but we continue today. We have to make sure, as that was revealed to Prophet ﷺ from Holy Qur'an:

يَا أَيُّهَا النَّاسُ قَدْ جَاءتْكُم مَّوْعِظَةٌ مِّن رَّبِّكُمْ وَشِفَاء لِّمَا فِي الصُّدُورِ وَهُدًى وَرَحْمَةٌ لِّلْمُؤْمِنِينَ

O Mankind! There has come to you a guidance from your Lord and a healing for (the diseases) in your hearts, and for those who believe, a guidance and a mercy. *(Surat Yunus, 10:57)*

"We sent with the Holy Qur'an what is a cure for human beings," means Holy Qur'an is the only cure that you get because its cure is not like normal medicine, when you take this tablet or that tablet and you will be cured but still it has side effects, still you get something that is not your sickness through these tablets you are taking. And Allah ﷻ said, "We sent through Holy Qur'an verses for curing humanity," for curing everyone, as Qur'an doesn't only cure physical sicknesses, but it also cures spiritual sicknesses and what normal tablets cannot resolve.

Prophet ﷺ was always concentrating on the cure for the soul and the ego. For physical *Allah Kareem*, but the main concern is to get rid of these bad manners, that is what is important. People don't touch on this subject as they don't like to open it and the *`ulama* don't like to open this subject.

He is saying:

فَمَا يَنْبَغِي أَنْ يُعْلَمَ ، أَنَّ الذُّنُوبَ وَالمَعَاصِيَ تَضُرُّ ، وَلَا بُدَّ أَنَّ ضَرَرَهَا فِي القَلْبِ كَضَرَرِ السُّمُومِ فِي الْأَبْدَانِ

He must know that sins and disobedience are very harmful not only physically, but also harmful for the heart. As poison harms the physical body, sins are like poison for our spirituality (that will veil us from seeing the Prophet [s]).

Who is the one who took Sayyidina Adam ؑ from Paradise? What was the poison that took Sayyidina Adam ؑ from Heaven? It was disobedience. Allah said, "Don't do that!" and he did that, "Don't eat from the tree!" and he ate from the tree. So what happened? That was the biggest poison on his soul, so Allah ﷻ took him out of Heaven and threw him on Earth. That is a sickness of the soul with no remedy and if you don't want to really try to clean your heart, it is very difficult.

How many *`ulama* around the world are doing *da`wah*, but is anything changing? Who are the best people after the prophets and the Sahaabah ؓ? What are the rewards Allah gives for someone who went on His Way and struggled on His Way and died in His Way? Is there any higher level than a *shaheed*, other than the Sahaabah ؓ, *awliya*, prophets? Look at what Allah ﷻ is saying about *shaheeds*.

Those Whom Allah Will Deem Liars and Throw in Hell

In *Sahih Muslim*, Abu Hurayrah ؓ said, "I heard Prophet ﷺ say:

عَنْ سُلَيْمَانَ بْنِ يَسَارٍ قَالَ تَفَرَّقَ النَّاسُ عَنْ أَبِي هُرَيْرَةَ فَقَالَ لَهُ نَاتِلُ أَهْلِ الشَّامِ أَيُّهَا الشَّيْخُ حَدِّثْنَا حَدِيثًا سَمِعْتَهُ مِنْ رَسُولِ اللَّهِ صَلَّى اللَّهُ عَلَيْهِ وَسَلَّمَ قَالَ نَعَمْ سَمِعْتُ رَسُولَ اللَّهِ صَلَّى اللَّهُ عَلَيْهِ وَسَلَّمَ يَقُولُ إِنَّ أَوَّلَ النَّاسِ يُقْضَى يَوْمَ الْقِيَامَةِ عَلَيْهِ رَجُلٌ اسْتُشْهِدَ فَأُتِيَ بِهِ فَعَرَّفَهُ نِعَمَهُ فَعَرَفَهَا قَالَ فَمَا عَمِلْتَ فِيهَا قَالَ قَاتَلْتُ فِيكَ حَتَّى اسْتُشْهِدْتُ قَالَ كَذَبْتَ وَلَكِنَّكَ قَاتَلْتَ لِأَنْ يُقَالَ جَرِيءٌ فَقَدْ قِيلَ ثُمَّ أُمِرَ بِهِ فَسُحِبَ عَلَى وَجْهِهِ حَتَّى أُلْقِيَ فِي النَّارِ وَرَجُلٌ تَعَلَّمَ الْعِلْمَ وَعَلَّمَهُ وَقَرَأَ الْقُرْآنَ فَأُتِيَ بِهِ فَعَرَّفَهُ نِعَمَهُ فَعَرَفَهَا قَالَ فَمَا عَمِلْتَ فِيهَا قَالَ تَعَلَّمْتُ الْعِلْمَ وَعَلَّمْتُهُ وَقَرَأْتُ فِيكَ الْقُرْآنَ قَالَ كَذَبْتَ وَلَكِنَّكَ تَعَلَّمْتَ الْعِلْمَ لِيُقَالَ عَالِمٌ وَقَرَأْتَ الْقُرْآنَ لِيُقَالَ هُوَ قَارِئٌ فَقَدْ قِيلَ ثُمَّ أُمِرَ بِهِ فَسُحِبَ عَلَى وَجْهِهِ حَتَّى أُلْقِيَ فِي النَّارِ وَرَجُلٌ وَسَّعَ اللَّهُ عَلَيْهِ وَأَعْطَاهُ مِنْ أَصْنَافِ الْمَالِ كُلِّهِ فَأُتِيَ بِهِ فَعَرَّفَهُ نِعَمَهُ فَعَرَفَهَا قَالَ فَمَا عَمِلْتَ فِيهَا قَالَ مَا تَرَكْتُ مِنْ سَبِيلٍ تُحِبُّ أَنْ يُنْفَقَ فِيهَا إِلَّا أَنْفَقْتُ فِيهَا لَكَ قَالَ كَذَبْتَ وَلَكِنَّكَ فَعَلْتَ لِيُقَالَ هُوَ جَوَادٌ فَقَدْ قِيلَ ثُمَّ أُمِرَ بِهِ فَسُحِبَ عَلَى وَجْهِهِ ثُمَّ أُلْقِيَ فِي النَّارِ

The first of people against whom Judgment will be pronounced on the Day of Resurrection will be a man who died a martyr. He will be brought and Allah will make known to him His favors and he will recognize them. (The Almighty) will say, "And what did you do about them?" He will say, "I fought for you until I died a martyr." He will say, "You have lied! You did but fight that it might be said (of you), 'He is courageous,' and so it was said." Then he will be ordered to be dragged along on his face until he is cast into Hellfire!

(Another) will be a man who has studied (religious) knowledge and has taught it and who used to recite the Qur'an. He will be brought and Allah will make known his His favors and he will recognize them. (The Almighty) will say, "And what did you do about them?" He will say. "I studied (religious) knowledge and I taught it and I recited the Qur'an for Your sake." He will say, "You have lied! You did but study (religious) knowledge that it might be said (of you), 'He is learned,' and you recited the Qur'an that it might be said (of you), 'He is a reciter,' and so it was said." Then he will be ordered to be dragged along on his face until he is cast into Hellfire!

(Another) will be a man whom Allah had made rich and to whom He had given all kinds of wealth. He will be brought and Allah will make known his His favors and he will recognize them. (The Almighty) will say, "And what did you do about them?" He will say, "I left no path (untrodden) in which You like money to be spent without spending in it for Your sake!" He will say, "You have lied! You did so that it might be said (of you), 'He is open-handed,' and so it was said." Then he will be ordered to be dragged along on his face until he is cast into Hellfire!" (Muslim, Tirmidhi, Nasa'i)

The first three people to be charged on the Day of Judgment, which means they symbolically represent the others: the first will be the *shaheed,* second the scholar, and third is the rich man. They are going to be the first to be asked. Do you like to be *shaheed,* yes or no? But listen to what he said: you don't want to be *shaheed* like this *shaheed* mentioned in *Sahih Muslim,* we want to be *shaheed* in a different way. The Prophet ﷺ said that the first to be called on the Day of Judgment is *astashahada fee sabeelillah,* a man who is martyred in the Way of Allah. *Fa ootiyi bihi fa `arafa ni`mahu fa `arafahaa,* Allah ﷻ will call him and show him His favors and say, *fa qaala maa `amilta feehaa,* "What did you do to deserve My favors?" and he will say, *fa qaala qaataltu feeka hatta qutilt,* "I went in Your Way until I died in Your Way."

So Allah ﷻ takes him and asks him what he did to deserve His favors. What will Allah ﷻ answer? *Qaala kadhibta,* "You have lied!" The *shaheed* is lying? Allah ﷻ turned the *shaheed* into a lying person! Therefore, we have to be very afraid and we have to be very careful with what we are doing and saying. May Allah ﷻ forgive us! Don't claim you are *shaheed* by doing suicide bombing and killing innocent people! Allah ﷻ said, "No, you are a liar! To Me you are not *shaheed.* You went to fight in order that people will say you are courageous, that people will honor you and your family. You are doing it for yourself to satisfy your ego." Since he satisfied his ego, Allah ﷻ will order angels to pull him on his face and throw him into Hellfire! That is for a '*shaheed.*' These are not my words, but the words of the Prophet ﷺ. We shall read it again:

The first of people against whom judgment will be pronounced on the Day of Resurrection will be a man who died a martyr. He will be brought and Allah will make known to him His favors and he will recognize them. (The Almighty) will say, "And what did you do about them?" He will say, "I fought for you until I died a martyr." He will say, "You have lied! You fought that it might be said (of you), 'He is courageous,' and so it was said. Then he will be ordered to be dragged along on his face until he is cast into Hellfire.

(Another) will be a man who has studied (religious) knowledge and has taught it and who used to recite the Qur'an. He will be brought and Allah will make known to his His favors and he will recognize them. (The Almighty) will say, "And what did you do about them?" He will say, "I studied (religious) knowledge and I taught it and I recited the Qur'an for Your sake." He will say, "You have lied! You studied (religious) knowledge that it might be said (of you), 'He is learned,' and you recited the Qur'an that it might be said (of you), 'He is a reciter,' and so it was said. Then he will be ordered to be dragged along on his face until he is cast into Hellfire.

(Another) will be a man whom Allah made rich and to whom He gave all kinds of wealth. He will be brought and Allah will make known to his His favors and he will recognize them. (The Almighty) will say, "What did you do about them?" He will say, "I left no path (untrodden) in which You like money to be spent without spending in it for Your sake." He will say, "You have lied! You did so that it might be said (of you), 'He is open-handed,' and so it was said. Then he will be ordered to be dragged along on his face until he is cast into Hellfire.

Allah ﷻ will throw him into Hellfire even though he says, "I am *shaheed*," but (he was) *shaheed* for his own ego. An example is when there was a war and Sayyidina `Ali ؓ had a sickness of the eye. In that time they used to first fight one-on-one and then the whole army fought. There was a big wrestler calling, "Where is that child, `Ali? Where is that one who is afraid of death?" And the Prophet ﷺ held Sayyidina `Ali ؓ back, telling him not to go as his eye was sick. That wrestler kept calling and finally Sayyidina `Ali ؓ said, "Let me go!" and the Prophet ﷺ said, "*Bismillahi 'r-Rahmani 'r-Raheem*," and put his ﷺ saliva on Sayyidina `Ali's ؓ eye, and then he was able to see up to *Qaaba Qawsayni aw Adnaa*! Allah ﷻ gave Sayyidina `Ali, *karram Allahu wajha wa `alayhi 's-salaam*, power to see what no one can see because of the saliva of Prophet ﷺ!

When the Prophet ﷺ is happy with someone he will grant him to reach *Qaaba Qawsayni aw Adnaa*. So if we do not disobey the Prophet ﷺ or Allah ﷻ, we will always be in ascension through our souls. The body might be sick, no problem; the body can be sick but the soul must not be sick.

The Prophet ﷺ said:

إنَّمَا بُعِثْتُ لأتَمِّمَ مَكَارِمَ الأخْلَاق

Innamaa bu`ithtu li utammimu makaarim al-akhlaaq.

I have been sent to perfect the best of conduct (your behavior and character).

(al-Bazzaar and Bukhari with different wording.)

The Prophet ﷺ is saying, "I was sent to complete the best of manners among people, to take away their bad behaviors." Do we have bad behavior? Is there anyone without bad behavior? No, we cannot claim to have good behavior!

The Prophet ﷺ used to say:

اللَّهُمَّ لَا تَكِلْنِي إِلَى نَفْسِي طَرْفَةَ عَيْنٍ وَلَا أقَلَّ مِنْ ذَلِكَ

Allahumma laa takilnee ila nafsee tarfat `aynin wa laa aqala min dhalika.

O Allah! Don't leave me to my ego for the blink of an eye or less.

When Sayyidina Abu Bakr as-Siddiq ؓ heard this, he disappeared and no one could find him. The Prophet ﷺ was looking and looking for him, until finally Sayyidina Jibreel ﷺ came and told the Prophet to look for him inside the *Ka`bah*, where Prophet found him crying.

The Prophet ﷺ said, "Why are you crying?"

Sayyidina Abu Bakr as-Siddiq ؓ said, "*Yaa Rasoolullah*! How can I not cry when you, the Perfect One, the Most Respected One, the One Who Reached Where No One has Reached, the One on Whom the Holy Qur'an has Been Revealed, said, 'O Allah! Don't leave me to my ego for the blink of an eye!' (If you are saying this), then what about me?"

And the Prophet ﷺ said, "*Yaa* Abu Bakr! Allah called you '*siddiq*,' so how is He going to punish you?"

Sayyidina Abu Bakr as-Siddiq ؓ said, "*Yaa Rasoolullah*! What if Allah takes that away from me on Judgment Day? Can anyone say to Him, 'What are you doing?'"

So they both sat there crying, until Jibreel ﷺ came and said to the Prophet ﷺ, "*Yaa Rasoolullah*! Tell him that Allah ﷻ has given him *bara`atun min an-naar*, guaranteed protection from Hellfire." Do we have that guarantee? We don't!

The second person to be judged on Judgment Day is a scholar or those who call themselves scholars, which is okay, but it depends on how much understanding they have. Didn't they read this Hadith of Prophet ﷺ? The second group to be judged on the Day of Judgment before the common people are those who consider themselves scholars and representatives of *awliyaullah*. We are just common people, but whatever you want to be asked about you will be asked. We are at the threshold of the Prophet ﷺ, asking for love of the Prophet ﷺ, love of Mawlana Shaykh Nazim and love of *awliyaullah*, that's it! We are not scholars, we have a book (to quote from) and we don't sit without a book because then our ego will say, "I don't need a book!" What did Grandshaykh ق say to me and my brother? He said, "Don't give a lecture without reading from my lectures; read one line and that will open." That is to show humbleness. Don't say, "I know," say, "No, I don't know." Look at that *`alim*.

Sayyidina Ali Defines True Martyrdom

Now let us complete the example of Sayyidina `Ali ؓ, the real example of martyrdom. He was fighting for Allah ﷻ, not like the one mentioned here.

Today they make videos of suicide bombers before they go and they have behind them a banner on which is written the name of the group, "We are this group and we are going fee sabeelillah to kill the *kuffaar*." They go to die and people begin spreading these videos around the world, saying, "Look! These are the martyrs." That is not martyrdom!

So after the Prophet ﷺ put his saliva, Sayyidina `Ali ؓ went out and fought the wrestler, turning him upside down and putting him on the ground. In that time if you got your opponent on the ground you can cut his neck! Then the enemy surrendered and Sayyidina `Ali ؓ was supposed to cut his neck, but right when he was about to cut his neck the man spat his face, then Sayyidina `Ali ؓ dropped his sword and said, "I will not kill you."

The man said, "Go ahead, you put me down!"

Sayyidina `Ali ؓ said, "No, I got angry when you spat on my face, so I cannot kill you as it will be to satisfy my ego, not for Islam. Now my ego wants to kill you, so I will not kill you."

The man said, "If this is Islam then I want to be Muslim!" and they both went to the Prophet ﷺ and he became Muslim.

When you fight for Allah ﷻ and His Prophet ﷺ it is worth it; you are a martyr if you fight if mentioned here in the Hadith. But if you fight for people to say you are courageous and to have your name put everywhere, that is not martyrdom and you will face Hellfire!

وَرَجُلٌ تَعَلَّمَ الْعِلْمَ وَعَلَّمَهُ وَقَرَأَ الْقُرْآنَ فَأُتِيَ بِهِ فَعَرَّفَهُ نِعَمَهُ فَعَرَفَهَا قَالَ فَمَا عَمِلْتَ فِيهَا قَالَ تَعَلَّمْتُ الْعِلْمَ وَعَلَّمْتُهُ وَقَرَأْتُ فِيكَ الْقُرْآنَ قَالَ كَذَبْتَ وَلَكِنَّكَ تَعَلَّمْتَ الْعِلْمَ لِيُقَالَ عَالِمٌ وَقَرَأْتَ الْقُرْآنَ لِيُقَالَ هُوَ قَارِئٌ فَقَدْ قِيلَ ثُمَّ أُمِرَ بِهِ فَسُحِبَ عَلَى وَجْهِهِ حَتَّى أُلْقِيَ فِي النَّارِ

The second to be judged: "A man who learned knowledge and learned Holy Qur'an and taught Holy Qur'an." Allah ﷻ will call him and show him the favors He gives to `ulama and will ask him, "What were you doing in order to deserve this?" He will say, "Yaa Rabbee! I learned knowledge, fiqh, Holy Qur'an, and taught it for Your sake." Allah ﷻ will say, "No, you did that for your own arrogance and for people to say you are an `alim so that people follow you. There was doubt in this knowledge that you spread."

Like now people are saying, "You are a big *`alim*, a doctor, PhD." When we were young, doctors were only medical. Now there are even doctors of plumbing and electricians, English-teaching doctors, French-teaching doctors. Can you believe in France I found Pakistanis that speak French, in Spain who speak Spanish and in Japan who speak Japanese? They are clever people!

So Allah ﷻ will say, "You did that for yourself, for people to call you *`alim*, not for Me; you took it from them to call you *`alim*, but I will not. Come!" and He will call the angels, *fa suhiba `alaa wajhihi wa `ulqiya fi 'n-naar*, "and he will be pulled on his face and be thrown into Hellfire."

Can you say, "I do *qasida*?" Can you say, "I teach Qur'an?" *Hasbun Allah wa ni`ma 'l-wakeel*! Forget about *qasida* and teaching Qur'an! Do you accept the opinion of other people? Do you get angry? You get angry too much!

The third to be judged:

وَرَجُلٌ وَسَّعَ اللَّهُ عَلَيْهِ وَأَعْطَاهُ مِنْ أَصْنَافِ الْمَالِ كُلِّهِ .

And a man to whom Allah has given a lot of wealth.

فَأُتِيَ بِهِ فَعَرَّفَهُ نِعَمَهُ فَعَرَفَهَا قَالَ فَمَا عَمِلْتَ فِيهَا ؟

Allah ﷻ will call him on the Day of Judgment to show him His favors and say, "What did you do to deserve this?"

قَالَ مَا تَرَكْتُ مِنْ سَبِيلٍ تُحِبُّ أَنْ يُنْفَقَ فِيهَا إِلَّا أَنْفَقْتُ فِيهَا لَكَ

He will say, "Yaa Rabbee! I looked in every way that You like for me to spend money and for helping and I spent it in Your Way!"

قَالَ كَذَبْتَ وَلَكِنَّكَ فَعَلْتَ لِيُقَالَ هُوَ جَوَادٌ فَقَدْ قِيلَ ثُمَّ أُمِرَ بِهِ فَسُحِبَ عَلَى وَجْهِهِ ثُمَّ أُلْقِيَ فِي النَّارِ

Allah will say, "You are a liar! You did that in order that they will say you are a generous person, to become famous and to satisfy your ego. So since they said what you wanted, you took what you deserve from people but you didn't get from Me. Take him to Hellfire and throw him in!"

O Muslims! This is a Hadith of the Prophet ﷺ, which explains the verse of Holy Qur'an:

وَقَدِمْنَا إِلَى مَا عَمِلُوا مِنْ عَمَلٍ فَجَعَلْنَاهُ هَبَاء مَّنثُورًا

And We shall turn to whatever deeds they did (in this life), and We shall make such deeds as floating dust scattered about. *(Surat al-Furqaan, 25:23)*

Allah ﷻ says, "On the Day of Judgment, We come to what they have done and make it as if to not exist, make it like ashes and throw it in their faces." What they have done of good is only for people to praise them. People today only do something good in order to be praised. That is why the Prophet ﷺ said, "Don't let your left hand see what your right hand gives." When you give, don't count it out, "Five dinars, ten dinars..." you know already how much it is. The Prophet ﷺ is saying don't let yourself know how much you give. So open the drawer, close your eyes, put in your hand and take without looking and counting. Are you doing this? No. So what did Sayyidina Abu Bakr ؓ say, according to Qutaada ؓ, one of his friends?

وَقَالَ قَتَادَةُ : بَلَغَنِي أَنَّ أَبَا بَكْرٍ قَالَ : لَيْتَنِي خُضْرَةٌ تَأْكُلُنِي الدَّوَابُّ .

I wish I were a blade of grass whose life ended with the grazing by some beast.

He said, "I wish that Allah made me grass that animals will eat me," which means, "I wish not to be, as I don't know if I will go to Hellfire and if Allah will be happy with me or not." That is Sayyidina Abu Bakr as-Siddiq ؓ, *awwala khulafaa 'r-raashidoon*, the first of the Rightly-Guided *Khalifahs*!

From the book, *Al-Jawaab al-Kaafee liman sa'ala `ala ad-daw`a ish-shafi`i, The Sufficient Answers for Those Who Asked about the Healing Medicine*, by Ibn Qayyim al-Jawziyya:

وَذَكَرَ عَنْهُ أَيْضًا أَنَّهُ كَانَ يَمْسِكُ بِلِسَانِهِ وَيَقُولُ : هَذَا الَّذِي أَوْرَدَنِي الْمَوَارِدَ ، وَكَانَ يَبْكِي كَثِيرًا ، وَيَقُولُ : ابْكُوا ، فَإِنْ لَمْ تَبْكُوا فَتَبَاكُوا .

وَكَانَ إِذَا قَامَ إِلَى الصَّلَاةِ كَأَنَّهُ عُودٌ مِنْ خَشْيَةِ اللَّهِ عَزَّ وَجَلَّ .

وَأُتِيَ بِطَائِرٍ فَقَلَبَهُ ثُمَّ قَالَ : مَا صِيدَ مِنْ صَيْدٍ ، وَلَا قُطِعَتْ شَجَرَةٌ مِنْ شَجَرَةٍ ، إِلَّا بِمَا ضَيَّعَتْ مِنَ التَّسْبِيحِ ، فَلَمَّا احْتَضَرَ ، قَالَ لِعَائِشَةَ : يَا بُنَيَّةُ ، إِنِّي أَصَبْتُ مِنْ مَالِ الْمُسْلِمِينَ هَذِهِ الْعَبَاءَةَ وَهَذِهِ الْحِلَابَ وَهَذَا الْعَبْدَ ، فَأَسْرِعِي بِهِ إِلَى ابْنِ الْخَطَّابِ ، وَقَالَ : وَاللَّهِ لَوَدِدْتُ أَنِّي كُنْتُ هَذِهِ الشَّجَرَةَ تُؤْكَلُ وَتُعْضَدُ .

And he used to cry and cry and cry too much and say to people, *ubkoo*, "Cry! If you cannot cry, poke your eyes to pretend that you are crying and make sure tears come out!" And whenever he stood up to pray he was like a stick of wood, very slim, afraid from Allah ﷻ; he became very thin when he prayed, "Yaa Rabbee! I don't want to be appearing. I am nothing!" And he used to say, "If I hunt or cut wood from a tree or do something for myself, that is time I lost for doing *tasbeeh*."

He was keeping what the Prophet ﷺ said, that the day is 24 hours: eight hours of work, eight hours of *`ibaadah* and eight hours of sleep. You cannot jump and take from one and make it less and the other part more. Eight hours *`ibaadah* means *Qiyaam al-Layl*, all the *sunnahs*, to sit with your family and raise them nicely and to give yourself rest and then to work. Today how many hours do we work: 16, 12, 14, 15 hours? And how many hours do we worship? Five minutes. Quickly, *y'Allah*, pray and finish and wrap it, and *y'Allah*! May Allah ﷻ keep us on the Right Way, not to be falling.

It is said that when Sayyidina `Umar ؓ was reading *Surat at-Toor*:

وَالطُّورِ وَكِتَابٍ مَّسْطُورٍفِي رَقٍّ مَّنشُورٍ وَالْبَيْتِ الْمَعْمُورِ وَالسَّقْفِ الْمَرْفُوعِ وَالْبَحْرِ
الْمَسْجُورِ إِنَّ عَذَابَ رَبِّكَ لَوَاقِعٌ

By the mount (of Revelation) and by a book inscribed in a scroll unfolded, and by the frequented House, and by the Heaven raised high, and (by) the sea filled (with fire)! Indeed, the punishment of your Lord will occur.

(Surat at-Toor, 52:1-7)

Allah ﷻ is giving an oath by all that is mentioned, by the *Ka`bah* and Tur Sinai and all these sacred places, that Allah's Punishment, *`adhaab*, is going to happen:

وَهَذَا عُمَرُ بْنُ الْخَطَّابِ قَرَأَ سُورَةَ الطُّورِ إِلَى أَنْ بَلَغَ : إِنَّ عَذَابَ رَبِّكَ لَوَاقِعٌ [سُورَةُ الطُّورِ : 77] فَبَكَى وَاشْتَدَّ بُكَاؤُهُ حَتَّى مَرِضَ وَعَادُوهُ .

[ص: 41] وَقَالَ لِابْنِهِ وَهُوَ فِي الْمَوْتِ : وَيْحَكَ ضَعْ خَدِّي عَلَى الْأَرْضِ عَسَاهُ أَنْ يَرْحَمَنِي ، ثُمَّ قَالَ : وَيْلُ أُمِّي ، إِنْ لَمْ يَغْفِرْ لِي (ثَلَاثًا) ، ثُمَّ قُضِيَ .

وَكَانَ يَمُرُّ بِالْآيَةِ فِي وِرْدِهِ بِاللَّيْلِ فَتُخِيفُهُ ، فَيَبْقَى فِي الْبَيْتِ أَيَّامًا يُعَادُ ، يَحْسَبُونَهُ مَرِيضًا ، وَكَانَ فِي وَجْهِهِ - رَضِيَ اللَّهُ عَنْهُ - خَطَّانِ أَسْوَدَانِ مِنَ الْبُكَاءِ .

وَقَالَ لَهُ ابْنُ عَبَّاسٍ ، مَصَّرَ اللَّهُ بِكَ الْأَمْصَارَ ، وَفَتَحَ بِكَ الْفُتُوحَ ، وَفَعَلَ ، فَقَالَ :
وَدِدْتُ أَنِّي أَنْجُو لَا أَجْرَ وَلَا وِزْرَ

And it is said that whenever Sayyidina `Umar ؓ read this ayah in which it says Allah's Punishment is happening, he would cry and begin to get severe panic attacks, severe sickness, until people began to come and check on him.

And this is the *khalifah*! From one verse they were crying! How many verses do we read a day and we are not crying? Look at the big difference!

And when Sayyidina `Umar was dying, he told his son, "Put my head on the floor directly."

When you put someone in the grave, you put his face towards *qiblah* and open the shroud and put something under the head.

He said, "Put my face directly on the sand, as maybe He will forgive me and send His Mercy on me." Then he said three times, "Woe to my mother if He doesn't forgive me! How much she is going to suffer if Allah doesn't forgive me!"

That was a saying in that time. Every day there is a *wird* that we recite." And in his *wird*, sometimes he passed by (read) an *ayah* and stayed in his house for days due to a panic attack, and the people used to think he must be ill."

Are we fearing? We don't remember, we don't remember! One verse of the Holy Qur'an made him cry and stay at home for many days!

He was crying so much, like a river, that the tears coming from his eyes made a mark on his face, two black lines, one from this eye and one from this eye. When Ibn `Abbas ؓ saw him in this situation he said to him, "May Allah open the doors of all countries on your hands."

That is why *futuhaat* of all countries was on the hands of Sayyidina `Umar ؓ!

وَهَذَا عُثْمَانُ بْنُ عَفَّانَ - رَضِيَ اللَّهُ عَنْهُ - كَانَ إِذَا وَقَفَ عَلَى الْقَبْرِ يَبْكِي حَتَّى تُبَلَّ لِحْيَتُهُ ، وَقَالَ : لَوْ أَنَّنِي بَيْنَ الْجَنَّةِ وَالنَّارِ لَا أَدْرِي إِلَى أَيَّتِهِمَا يُؤْمَرُ بِي ، لَاخْتَرْتُ أَنْ أَكُونَ رَمَادًا قَبْلَ أَنْ أَعْلَمَ إِلَى أَيَّتِهِمَا أَصِيرُ .

Similarly, Sayyidina `Uthman ؓ used to come in front of the grave of the Prophet ﷺ and any other holy grave and used to cry until his beard became soaked from tears! He used to say, "If I was between Paradise and Hellfire, I *don't know which one Allah will tell me to enter, either Hell or Paradise. No one can decide except Him! I wish to be ashes at that time, before I know where I am going."*

Inna `adhaaba rabbaka la waaqi`a, "Allah's Punishment is happening." I am not opening this (subject) to frighten anyone, but Allah ﷻ said in the Holy Qur'an:

ومَا نُرْسِلُ بِالآيَاتِ إِلاَّ تَخْوِيفًا

We only send the Signs by way of terror (and warning from evil).

(Surat al-'Israa, 17:59)

There is a hidden meaning (in this *ayah*), "We don't send the verses except to make people frightened." After this scary situation, Grandshaykh, may Allah bless his soul, said, as many scholars and *awliyaullah* have said, that from this verse they understand that Allah sends these verses to make people frightened, but on Judgment Day His Rahmah is over that. As in this life they put a law to keep you on the right track or else you might run right and left, so Allah is giving these *ayaat* in order to keep people on the right track, but on the Day of Judgment:

سَبَقَتْ رَحْمَتِي على غَضَبِي

Sabaqat rahmatee `alaa ghadabee.

When Allah completed the Creation, He wrote in His Book which is with Him on His Throne, "My Mercy overrides My Anger."

(Narrated by Abu Hurayrah. Sahih Bukhari)

Wa maa arsalnaaka illaa rahmatan li 'l-`alameen,* and we know of many *ahadith* of Prophet ﷺ that state how he is going to make *shafaa` for his *ummah*:

So on the Day of Judgment, Allah's Mercy will override His Anger and we also know that the Prophet ﷺ is going to intercede for his *ummah*. But we have this problem: don't take Rahmatullah for granted! Why was Sayyidina Abu Bakr as-Siddiq ؓ afraid? Do you know what he said? "Nothing but my tongue has put me in problems." He considered his tongue put him in problems. He also used to say, *wadtu an akoona sha`aratun fee janb `abdan mu'min,* "I wish I were a hair on the body of a *mu'min*!" which means (in that case) there would be no judgment for him. If Sayyidina Abu Bakr as-

Siddiq ﷺ is saying, "When I open my mouth and talk, this is what throws me into problems," today can you see anyone whose tongue is frozen? They sell dry ice in the market, we have to put it in our mouth in order to freeze our tongue, otherwise no one here or anywhere, none of us can guarantee what our tongue might say!

May Allah ﷻ forgive us and may Allah ﷻ bless us.

Wa min Allahi 't-tawfiq, bi ḥurmati 'l-ḥabīb, bi ḥurmati 'l-Fātiḥah.

And with Allah is success. For the sake of the Beloved, for his sake we recite the opening chapter of Holy Qur'an.

Stunning Examples of the Sahaabah

A'ūdhu billāhi min ash-Shayṭāni 'r-rajīm. Bismillāhi' r-Raḥmāni 'r-Raḥīm.
Nawaytu 'l-arbā'īn, nawaytu 'l-'itikāf, nawaytu'l-khalwah, nawaytu 'l-'uzlah,
nawaytu 'r-riyāḍa, nawaytu 's-sulūk, lillāhi Ta'alā fī hādhā 'l-masjid.
Atī'ūllāha wa atī'ū 'r-Rasūla wa ūlī 'l-amri minkum.
Obey Allah, obey the Prophet, and obey those in authority among you. (4:59)

Dastūr, madad yā Sulṭān al-Awlīyā, Mawlana Shaykh Nazim al-Haqqani ق.
Dastūr, madad yā Sulṭān al-Awlīyā, Mawlana Shaykh 'AbdAllah ad-Daghestani ق.

We are taking some *ahadith,* sayings that have been mentioned in many different sources, and we are taking from the book *"Al-Jawaab al-kaafee liman sa'ala `ala ad-daw`a ish-shaafee, The Sufficient Answers for Those Who Asked about the Healing Medicine,"* by Ibn Qayyim al-Jawziyya, who was a student of Ibn Taymiyya. We are taking from there because it is from their own things that they accept, in order that we can build on it as *Ahlu 's-Sunnah wa 'l-Jama`ah,* lovers of Prophet ﷺ.

We are mentioning about *du`as* and we have about ten or twelve lectures on the importance of *du`a* in curing, what we shouldn't do in order to be saved in *dunya* and *Akhirah,* and how the Sahaabah ﷺ used to look at what the Prophet ﷺ was saying to them and build on that with their own sayings and their own statements. In the last lecture, we mentioned about Sayyidina Abu Bakr as-Siddiq ﷺ, Sayyidina `Umar Farooq ﷺ and Sayyidina `Uthmaan Ibn `Affan ﷺ and what they have said.

Du`a saves you from the poison of *Akhirah* and poison of *dunya,* if we can call it poison, through which different kinds of negative energy affect your body and your system. Also, the poison of *Akhirah* are things that affect your *Akhirah,* the poison that you build up on your soul from sins. So the sins that you do in *dunya* will affect your *dunya* and *Akhirah.* The Sahaabah ﷺ tried to be careful and to run away from it and they wished many things in order not to see that kind of poison that we will be dressed with in *Akhirah.*

We mentioned about Sayyidina Abu Bakr as-Siddiq ﷺ and I am not going to repeat it, but he used to cry a lot and say, "O Allah! I wished You had made me a hair on the body of a *mu'min,"* meaning, "a hair for me is enough in the body of a *mu'min* because that hair will not be judged on the Day of Judgment as it is already in the body of a *mu'min*." That means, "I wish I will not be left to my ego, as Prophet ﷺ said, 'O Allah! Don't leave me to my ego for the blink of an eye!'"

So Sayyidina Abu Bakr as-Siddiq ؓ used to say the same that he heard from the Prophet ﷺ, and he used to say, "*Ibkoo*, cry, and if you are not able to cry, then *tabaakoo*, try to cry to your self," as Allah's Punishment is not easy.

And Abu Qatada ؓ said that Sayyidina Abu Bakr as-Siddiq ؓ said, "I wish to be vegetation that animals eat me," meaning, "I wish not to exist!"

Sayyidina `Umar ؓ said to his son, "When I die, put my face directly on the soil." Today they don't put it directly on soil, but they put it in a coffin and the coffin is first on the soil, then the sand. He said, "Put my face directly on the ground and perhaps with this humiliation that I do to myself Allah ﷻ will forgive me."

Sometimes when he was reading Holy Qur'an at night and passed by a verse that would make him cry, he cried for several days and would get sick and not leave his house for many days until he felt better. So the verses of Holy Qur'an as he was passing through them, it was terrifying him from Allah's `*adhaab*, Punishment, which we have explained.

And Sayyidina `Uthmaan ؓ, as we explained, said, "If I was between *Jannah* and *Naar* waiting for Allah's Judgment on me, at that moment I wish to be ashes, not to exist anywhere, because I don't know what Allah's Judgment will be, so I wish I am non-existing," meaning, "I am like ashes."

The Wisdom of Avoiding Long-Term Planning

It is said that Sayyidina `Ali ؓ used to fear so much when he read the Holy Qur'an and all his life he was afraid, worried that Allah is not happy with him. He was worried about two issues that we have to put in front of our eyes. Today, people are not living for their day and very few people say, "I am living for this day, I don't have something for tomorrow." We could say, "Living for today," meaning they don't have any thinking about tomorrow. Sayyidina `Ali ؓ used to say, "I am afraid of two, *tool al-amal*, looking too far in the future, that I wish to live so much that I want to have all this in my future life."

Today everyone feels that they have to plans for ten years ahead, or twenty years ahead; companies today make twenty year plans, countries plan for twenty years. Perhaps you die, or perhaps a tsunami comes and takes you all? So how are you planning and Allah might call you at any moment? What you really need to plan is for your *Akhirah*, and not for your *dunya*. That is why Sahaabah ﷺ used to live for the day. And he said, "*Toola al-amal* makes me to think too much in the future, that is a danger on me, and I always try hard not to think like that."

There was one *wali* in Damascus, Shaam, and I have mentioned that before, he used to live his day. Any gifts that came to him during the day, he could not sleep without giving it out. Many people might give him something as a gift or *sadaqa* to distribute, but we are talking about what he owns, the gifts he has to make sure it is being given out. One day he came to his house and he already advised his daughter, "Distribute it if I am late, give everything out. One day he came to the house, he made *wudu*, prayed two *raka`ats* and went to bed, but he was not able to sleep. He knew that if he was not able to sleep it meant there is something from *dunya* in the house above their needs. Today, what do you need to live your life? A mattress, if you want a mattress. Prophet ﷺ and the Sahaabah ﷺ used to sleep on a mattress of straw. Now they tell you there is a mattress from foam and springs, and a mattress you could buy for $5, now you can buy for $3,000! And now not only that, they have mattresses with electricity, it heats up and goes up and goes down the way you like, and they say it takes your body pattern and it functions similarly. They used to sleep on a straw mattress!

What was the Prophet's food? Bread, and in the morning a cup of hot water with one spoon of honey. Do we do that? We need coffee, tea and we need breakfast. He took one cup of hot water with honey and at noon time before lunch, he took seven dates and one cup of milk. Before *Maghrib*, he took one piece of broken bread, and it was very hard and mainly with olive oil and vinegar he dipped it in salt and ate it. This was the main meal and some days only three dates. This is doing for *Akhirah*. For *dunya* you need what all of us are falling into, the trap of Shaytan. They have everything and planning also what you have to save in your freezer and fridge and everything, in case if something happened what to do. So Sayyidina `Ali ﷺ used to be afraid from that.

So that *wali* was checking and he was not able to sleep, (and he knew) there is something from *dunya* in the house that had not been given out. He woke his daughter and asked, "What do we have in the house that has not been distributed today?"

She said, "*W'Allahi*! O my father, we have nothing. I gave everything out, whatever came of food or gifts or cloth I distributed, anything that came like wheat or chickpeas or lentils, I gave out. There is nothing."

So they lived for their day, day-by-day. The next day, Allah Kareem, they didn't think about the next day. Do we think of next day? Too much thinking about next day; we don't think of today because today we know already we have prepared for it like a month ago! We think about tomorrow.

وَلَا تَقُولَنَّ لِشَيْءٍ إِنِّي فَاعِلٌ ذَٰلِكَ غَدًا إِلَّا أَن يَشَاءَ اللَّهُ

And never say of anything, "Indeed, I will do that tomorrow," except (when adding), "If Allah wills." *(Surat al-Kahf, 18:23)*

"Don't say about something, 'I am going to do this tomorrow.' Leave it to Allah." It might be if you leave it to Allah, Allah will give you millions more than what you planned.

So that man said, "No, no there must be something in the house." Then she remembered that someone had brought them a leg of lamb and she had put it above the cupboard and she forgot about it, so he took it down and cut it into pieces and went out. Who was on the streets? Cats and dogs; who else is out after midnight? What to do, knock on doors of people's houses? So he gave it to them and went home and he was able to sleep. Before *Fajr* he woke up and made *wudu* and prayed Qiyaam al-Layl and was going to the *masjid* and all those dogs and cats were following him to the *masjid*, because they were happy with him and they were loyal to him because he gave to them; a dog is loyal when you give him something, is it not? Allah gave to us everything.

وَلَقَدْ كَرَّمْنَا بَنِي آدَمَ وَحَمَلْنَاهُمْ فِي الْبَرِّ وَالْبَحْرِ وَرَزَقْنَاهُم مِّنَ الطَّيِّبَاتِ وَفَضَّلْنَاهُمْ عَلَى كَثِيرٍ مِّمَّنْ خَلَقْنَا تَفْضِيلاً

We have honored the Children of Adam, provided them with transport on land and sea, given them for sustenance things good and pure, and conferred on them special favors above a great part of Our Creation. (Surat al-'Israa, 17:70)

"We have honored the Children of Adam and carried them in lands and seas and provided them from the most delicious that they want to eat." So we must be loyal to Allah ﷻ by obeying Him. That is why Sayyidina `Ali ؓ said, "I am worried if I am not loyal to obey Allah and obey His Prophet ﷺ and tool al-amal, looking for what you need to do for the future will take you away from loyalty to the Prophet ﷺ and loyalty to Allah, because you are going to be loyal to yourself first when are looking for what you are going to do in the future, not loyal to what Allah has given to you and depending on Allah ﷻ, not depending on your ego, on yourself." So he was worried that this might happen and he could not deal with it because the ego always asks you, "What are you going to do tomorrow? What kind of work do you want to do?" Today, big companies do 2020 plans or 2030 plans; everything today is built contrary to what Allah likes.

مَا أُرِيدُ مِنْهُم مِّن رِّزْقٍ وَمَا أُرِيدُ أَن يُطْعِمُونِ إِنَّ اللَّهَ هُوَ الرَّزَّاقُ ذُو الْقُوَّةِ الْمَتِينُ

No sustenance do I require of them, nor do I require that they should feed Me. Indeed, it is Allah who is the (Continual) Provider, the Firm Possessor of Strength. (Surat adh-Dhaariyat, 51:57-58)

"I don't want from them any provision! Allah is the Provider of whatever they want."

إِنَّ اللَّهَ اشْتَرَىٰ مِنَ الْمُؤْمِنِينَ أَنفُسَهُمْ وَأَمْوَالَهُم بِأَنَّ لَهُمُ الْجَنَّةَ

Indeed, Allah has purchased from the believers their lives and their properties; (in exchange) for that they will have Paradise. (Surat at-Tawbah, 9:111)

Allah bought from those believers everything, He took from them their lives! *Ashtara* means, "He bought." Allah ﷻ is saying, "Give Me this, I will give you Paradise; give me struggle in *dunya* in My Way and I will give you Paradise." Allah bought from believers themselves and their wealth in order that He gives them Paradise.

Today, what are we doing? We are not selling to Allah ﷻ, but we are selling to Shaytan; we are selling him ourselves, saying, "Take it!"

"Eh, how I can take it? You have to think about what is going to happen to you after a hundred years."

"A hundred years, *Allah Kareem*!"

"No, you have to keep thinking."

So you begin to fight it, because when you think you need something you fight for it. That's why countries are fighting with each other, because everyone wants the chair.

هَزَمَ الأحْزَابَ وَحْدَهُ

Wa hazama 'l-ahzaaba wahdah.

He is the One that demolished all different parties. *(Sahih Bukhari)*

كُلُّ حِزْبٍ بِمَا لَدَيْهِمْ فَرِحُونَ

Kullu hizbin bima ladayhim farihoon.

Each party rejoices in that which is with itself. (Surat al-Mu'minoon, 23:53)

These parties in politics, *wa hazama 'l-ahzaaba wahdah,* "Allah destroys these parties by Himself," *Kullu hizbin bima ladayhim farihoon,* "Every party is happy with what they have." They are not happy with Allah ﷻ, they are happy with their Shaytan! So Sayyidina `Ali ؓ was worried. He said, "I am worried thinking about the future as I am here today and after one minute I might not be existing, I might die."

Today they sell you a house and you take out a thirty-year loan. They know you might not live thirty years, you might die after five years, and then they take the house because the wife cannot continue paying. They take everything from you, and they made it thirty years in order to get three times the value of the house; if you buy the house for $300,000 you pay a million dollars over thirty years! So everything (in their way) is built on wealth, on money and on Shaytan, while anything built on imaan takes you to *Akhirah* and saves you there. Can you buy *hasanaat* with money? Can you go to him and say, "Can you send me some *hasanaat*, I will give you that money?" How? He does not have a guarantee of *hasanaat*. Everyone, all of us, we cannot guarantee that we have something good or that we are doing something good. How am I going to give him what I don't own? So how am I going to go to him and say, "Give me ten *hasanaat*"? What is the value? If you put ten *hasanaat* on one side of the Scale and the whole value of *dunya* from yourself on the other, the ten *hasanaat* side is heavier! So how much do you want to sell it for? You cannot know, so what can you sell? And today they don't sell us anything except plans in air, from which there is no benefit. What has benefit? Only to obey Allah ﷻ and obey Prophet ﷺ! The Sahaabah ؓ knew that.

Sayyidina `Ali ؓ said, "Tool al-amal." It means that you want to do for the future, and that makes you forget about *Akhirah,* because 'tool al-amal' is to live long and you look forward to get a lot of things in the future. So you are building for your future; for example, the average lifespan is seventy-five years and you are thirty years of age, so you are building your hope for forty or fifty years ahead. You might die tomorrow and lose everything and you lose your *Akhirah,* but if you build your hope looking to build in *Akhirah,* that is acceptable. You can do that because it comes under the chapter of "Obey Allah and obey Prophet ﷺ." He said, "Tool al-amal, I am worried because *wa yunsee al-akhirah,* it makes you forget about your *Akhirah.*"

Wa amman tibaa al-hawaa fa yasudu `ala 'l-haqq, "And the second thing is to follow your desires." Following desires takes you away from Truth, because desires are never on truth. Bad desires, are always what Shaytan is pushing into your mind to do. Good desires are very rare to come to your mind. For example, a good desire is not only to pray *Zhuhr,* like we just prayed *Zhuhr,* but to come to your mind to pray a hundred *raka`ats*! Do you do that? Or it comes to your mind to pray fifty *raka`ats.* Do you do that? Or to read Holy Qur'an. If you open Holy Qur'an to read, hundreds of phone calls come. So what do you need to do? Unplug the telephone; that is a good desire. Do you turn off the phone? When I am giving *khutbah* on *Jumu`ah,* I am seeing people sending text messages to each other; the telephones are on vibration and as soon as it vibrates, people open the phone and are checking. (According to Shari`ah) if you carry a stone or a *masbaha* when the imam is on the *minbar,* your prayer is false! Today too many people even speak with each other and the *khutbah* is part of the prayer; it is the two *raka`ats* of prayer. You cannot even move in *Jumu`ah,* your focus must be on the imam, the *khateeb*!

So Sayyidina `Ali ؓ is worried to follow bad desires, *ittib`a al-hawwa,* that will take him away from *haqq.* O Human Beings! He said, "This *dunya* is moving, finishing its days, and *Akhirah,* heavenly life is coming." So then which one you have to work for? *Akhirah.* I am not saying this to these people here or people who go to *masaajid. Alhamdulillah,* may Allah's Beautiful Names and Attributes be on all of you as it is not easy to come from far distances to spend some time and go back. That is against the Desire of the Self, *ittib`a al-hawwaa*, as Sayyidina `Ali ؑ was saying.

And he said, "For everyone there is a child; *dunya* has its children, *Akhirah* has its children. Be from the children of *Akhirah*, not from children of *dunya*." And those who go for good cause to learn in *masaajid* are 'Children of *Akhirah*,' and don't fall into *ittiba` al-hawwaa*, the Desire of the Self. May Allah keep us safe here and there, wherever they are.

But too many today have programs called "leadership programs," to teach them to be leaders, injecting them with a full injection of arrogance and pride. That is it! I am not saying not to teach them leadership, but teach them leadership with humbleness, because good leadership is a humble leadership, just like Sayyidina `Umar ؑ was disguising himself, going around carrying sacks of food on his back and checking which houses are in need and giving to the poor. And one lady complained to him, "I wish that Sayyidina `Umar learns from you!" So speaking to leadership, there are also leadership using any possible way to put themselves on top of everyone, from people of *dunya* and from people of *Akhirah*. They don't care if they divide the community, but if they find a chance to sit on the chair— and that is what they are trying to do in every *tariqah* and especially this *tariqah*, the Naqshbandi- Haqqani Sufi Order! They are trying to divide, *ittib`a al-hawwaa*, they are following their bad desires. If I say what I have heard from many, many people about what they are trying to do to divide this community, some people in different countries are trying to divide the community and make different branches. What is the benefit? Then I will tell you what will happen at the end: if you continue to do that, then each will take his branch and go with it and no one will accept what you try to portray that this one is responsible and the other one is not responsible. "You follow this one! Leadership will be this one or that one." It is not going to happen. No, there will be a big division into hundreds of branches in the Naqshbandi-Haqqani Sufi Order!

May Allah ﷻ guide them all and guide us all not to reach that way, to check people, asking them, "With whom are you? With which division are you?" in different countries and you promote one against others and try to make a huge *sharkh*, fracture. If you fracture a bone, it needs one month or six weeks to heal, but these fractures will never heal!

In the Muslim community today there is a fracture. In the Salafi community there is a fracture, they are fighting with each other; in *Ahlu 's-*

*Sunnah wa 'l-Jama`ah* there are fractures; in Shi`a *madhhab* there is a fracture; in the Sufi's there are fractures; in Naqshbandis there are fractures. And who is going to take responsibility in front of Allah ﷻ and His Prophet ﷺ? You are only trying to promote *fitna*, you are not trying to keep *fitna* dormant or eliminate it. When you ask someone coming at the door of *awliyaullah*, "Which group are you following?" or you promote one group against another, then you know that you are doing something against Allah ﷻ and His Prophet ﷺ, and against the shaykh that you are following! We have to tell you that in *dunya* there are 124,000 shaykhs. There is a sultan and everyone thinks his shaykh is a sultan, so we believe that Mawlana Shaykh Nazim ق is our sultan. So don't destroy that way of belief in people!

May Allah ﷻ guide us towards *Akhirah*, as Sayyidina `Ali ؓ said, "For *dunya* there are children and for *Akhirah* there are children." Don't be the children of *dunya*, and we are running after it only for collecting from here and there things that *awliyaullah* never touch. You are touching it for fame or for a chair? And Allah knows the hearts and who is doing what. May Allah forgive us and forgive you. Be from the children of *Akhirah* and not from the children of this life!

Today there is *`amal bi laa hisaab, `amal* with no judgment. Whatever you do today you don't feel any punishment or reward, you will not get any answer, but tomorrow in *Akhirah* there is no *`amal*, but there is *hisaab*, judgment! So we have to choose.

I will read that Hadith and will not explain it today, but one day *inshaa-Allah*. Allah is Great! Imam Ahmad ق said in his *Musnad*, and in this book a majority of the Hadith, if not all, have a strong *sanad*:

عن عبد الرحمن بن جبير بن نفير عن أبيه قال: لما فتحت قبرص فُرق بين أهلها، فبكى بعضهم إلى بعض، فرأيت أبا الدرداء جالساً وحده يبكي، فقلت: يا أبا الدرداء ما يبكيك في يوم أعز الله فيه الإسلام وأهله، فقال: ويحك يا جبير ما أهون الخلق على الله إذا أضاعوا أمره، بينما هي أمة قاهرة ظاهرة لهم الملك، تركوا أمر الله فصاروا إلى ما ترى.

Lammaa futihat qubrus fariqat bayna ahluhaa, fa bakaa ba`duhum illa b`ad, fa rayatu aba dardaee jalasan wahdahu yabkee. Fa kultu yaa aba dardaee maa yubkeek fee yawmin a`azallahu feehi 'l-islama wa ahluh. Fa qaala wayhaka yaa jubayr maa ahwana 'l-khalqa `ala-'Llaahi `azza wa jalla idhaa adaa`oo amrahu baynamaa hiya ummatun qaahiratun zhahiratun lahumu 'l-mulk tarakoo amrullah fa saaroo ila maa taraa.

I will keep it in Arabic and translate it in English, to correctly understand every word we are saying. I will leave it until another time to explain it. It is in the book, *Al-Jawaab al-Kaafee liman sa'ala `ala ad-daw`a ish-shafi`i*, page 66.

May Allah ﷻ forgive us and may Allah ﷻ bless us.

Wa min Allahi 't-tawfiq, bi ḥurmati 'l-ḥabīb, bi ḥurmati 'l-Fātiḥah.

And with Allah is success. For the sake of the Beloved, for his sake we recite the opening chapter of Holy Qur'an.

Amazing Sayings of the Sahaabah

Aʿūdhu billāhi min ash-Shayṭāni 'r-rajīm. Bismillāhi' r-Raḥmāni 'r-Raḥīm.
Nawaytu 'l-arbāʿīn, nawaytu 'l-ʿitikāf, nawaytu'l-khalwah, nawaytu 'l-ʿuzlah,
nawaytu 'r-riyāḍa, nawaytu 's-sulūk, lillāhi Taʿalā fi hādhā 'l-masjid.
Atīʿūllāha wa atīʿū 'r-Rasūla wa ūlī 'l-amri minkum.
Obey Allah, obey the Prophet, and obey those in authority among you. (4:59)

Dastūr, madad yā Sulṭān al-Awlīyā, Mawlana Shaykh Nazim al-Haqqani ق.
Dastūr, madad yā Sulṭān al-Awlīyā, Mawlana Shaykh ʿAbdAllah ad-Daghestani ق.

What harms the body is *al-ma`aasiyya,* the sins, like if you give an injection to a sick person and give him poison on top of that, he will die immediately. Sins are like an injection to a weak body, so when you get an injection of poisonous sins it will affect your body. So Allah ﷻ has revealed the cure for that when He revealed:

قُلْ يَا عِبَادِيَ الَّذِينَ أَسْرَفُوا عَلَى أَنفُسِهِمْ لَا تَقْنَطُوا مِن رَّحْمَةِ اللَّهِ إِنَّ اللَّهَ يَغْفِرُ الذُّنُوبَ جَمِيعًا إِنَّهُ هُوَ الْغَفُورُ الرَّحِيمُ

Qul yaa `ibaadiya alladheena asrafoo `alaa anfusihim laa taqnatoo min rahmatillaahi inna Allaaha yaghfiru 'dh-dhunooba jamee`an innahu huwa 'l-ghafooru 'r-raheem.

Say, "O my Servants who have transgressed against their souls! Despair not of the Mercy of Allah, for Allah forgives all sins for He is Oft-Forgiving, Most Merciful." *(Surat al-Zumar, 39:53)*

Forgiveness is the way Allah ﷻ has put on Himself to help His servants; that's why He said:

وَلَوْ أَنَّهُمْ إِذ ظَّلَمُوا أَنفُسَهُمْ جَاؤُوكَ فَاسْتَغْفَرُوا اللَّهَ وَاسْتَغْفَرَ لَهُمُ الرَّسُولُ لَوَجَدُوا اللَّهَ تَوَّابًا رَّحِيمًا

Wa law annahum idh zhalamoo anfusahum ja'ooka f 'astaghfaroollaaha w 'astaghfara lahumu 'r-rasoolu la-wajadoo 'Llaaha tawwaaba 'r-raheema.

If they had only, when they were unjust to themselves, come to you and asked Allah's forgiveness, and the Messenger had asked forgiveness for them, they would have found Allah indeed Oft-Returning, Most Merciful.

(Surat an-Nisa, 4:64)

"*Yaa* Muhammad! Say to My servants that they have gone so far in *ma`aasiyy*, sins, that *laa taqnatoo min rahmatillah*, don't lose hope of Allah's Mercy!" If Allah is putting this on Himself, what is our duty? To also forgive those who did bad to us, because when we forgive them Allah will cure us from our sicknesses. When you forgive Allah forgives, and when you forgive someone Allah forgives you! And our duty is to ask forgiveness from Allah ﷻ.

So, *ma`aasiyy*, sins, worried many Sahaabah ؓ and scholars. I will quote Abu Darda ؓ (from *Al-Jawaab al-kaafee liman sa'ala `ala ad-daw`a ish-shaafee, The Sufficient Answers for Those Who Asked about the Healing Medicine* by Ibn Qayyim al-Jawziyya), who said:

وَهَذَا أَبُو الدَّرْدَاءِ كَانَ يَقُولُ : إِنَّ أَشَدَّ مَا أَخَافُ عَلَى نَفْسِي يَوْمَ الْقِيَامَةِ أَنْ يُقَالَ لِي : يَا أَبَا الدَّرْدَاءِ ، قَدْ عَلِمْتَ ، فَكَيْفَ عَمِلْتَ فِيمَا عَلِمْتَ ؟ وَكَانَ يَقُولُ : لَوْ تَعْلَمُونَ مَا أَنْتُمْ لَاقُونَ بَعْدَ الْمَوْتِ لَمَا أَكَلْتُمْ طَعَامًا عَلَى شَهْوَةٍ ، وَلَا شَرِبْتُمْ شَرَابًا عَلَى شَهْوَةٍ ، وَلَا دَخَلْتُمْ بَيْتًا تَسْتَظِلُّونَ فِيهِ ، وَلَخَرَجْتُمْ إِلَى الصُّعُدَاتِ تَضْرِبُونَ صُدُورَكُمْ ، وَتَبْكُونَ عَلَى أَنْفُسِكُمْ ، وَلَوَدِدْتُ أَنِّي شَجَرَةٌ تُعْضَدُ ثُمَّ تُؤْكَلُ .

Ashaddu maa akhaaf, "The thing I get afraid from most on Judgment Day." Who is not afraid on that day? I don't know, I think we are not afraid as we are still falling into sins, meaning that we are not learning our lesson. But we say, "*Yaa Rabbee*! We are weak servants, forgive us!" We cannot be like Sahaabah ؓ who know how to address their *du`as*! He says, "The thing I fear most is that I will be called on Judgment Day, '*Yaa* Abu Darda! You learned everything; the Prophet ﷺ taught you everything! You are a scholar, a Sahaabi ؓ, a *wali*, a star in dark nights for people to follow. You knew *ahadith* of the Prophet ﷺ and you were raised by the Prophet ﷺ.

Fa kayfa `amilta fee maa `alimta, what have you done through what you learned? You learned everything and so you must act on what you learned. Did you act on what you learned?'"

All of us are learning to make *istighfaar*. Are we making *istighfaar*? All of us have been ordered to obey Allah ﷻ and His Prophet ﷺ. Are we obeying Allah and His Prophet ﷺ? This is a Sahaabi ؓ, a Companion of the Prophet ﷺ who is worried. He is worried that he will be asked, "Did you do what you have learned?"

Abu Darda ؓ used to say, *law ta`alamoona maa antum laaqoona ba`ad al-mawti lamaa akaltum ta`amaa `alaa shahwa*, "If you knew what you are going to see when you die, you will never eat the food you desire."

Allahu Akbar! Today, we were checking our ego and our desire yesterday. These people in the *masjid* wanted to offer us food and they did offer us food and they gave us a package. Where is that package? It disappeared. They offered to feed us at the mosque, but all of us said, "How are we going to eat here like this!" One said, "Kebab!" and the other said, "Kebab!" Out of love they wanted to offer something. What is the difference between the kebab that they offer in the restaurant and the rice offered in the *masjid*? The rice has *barakah* and the kebab has no *barakah* because it is in an open house while the other is in a *masjid*.

With kebab you only taste the food you desire, but after five minutes it is gone as the taste is from the beginning of the tongue to end of the tongue, no further; after that it goes to the esophagus. It is the same, like people who get food through the tube, is there any taste? But they survive. Is it different? So now when you eat kebab, who is eating? Say! Who is eating when you eat kebab? Your desires are the ones eating! So he is saying that if they know what they are going to meet after death, they would never eat from their desires. That means they eat whatever they find, if they like it or not. When Prophet ﷺ didn't find food at home he put vinegar, olive oil, dry bread and mixed it and ate, or dates—it's a famous Hadith—and he was tying his stomach with stones from hunger. Are we doing this? We never slept a day in hunger! *Alhamdulillah*, every day we have the best food.

So what did Abu Darda ؓ say?

Inna ashadda maa akhaafa `alaa nafsee yawm al-qiyaamah an yuqaala lee yaa Aba Darda: Qad `alimta fa kayfa `amilta fee maa `alimta. Wa kaana yaqool: law ta`alamoona ma antum laaqoona ba`ad al-mawti lamaa akaltum ta`amaa `alaa shahwa. Finished! It means you cannot eat any desirable food that you like. Eat what you are offered and don't praise or raise your ego by saying, "I don't eat this!" If you go to a Muslim or *mu'min's* house after a prayer and he offers you food, even if you have high blood pressure and there is a lot of salt, if you eat it, it will be a cure from disease. Or sugar, people say, "I can't touch sugar!" No, eat it! That's *barakah*. You didn't ask for it, Allah gave it to you so you must eat it.

Wa laa sharibtum sharaaban `alaa shahwa, "And you will never drink anything according to your desires." What is this 'smoothie'? I never heard anything of this except in this place. What is a smoothie? Ice, you are eating ice! They color it and give you water to drink and charge you for a smoothie. "We have to go to Starbucks!" to pay $5 or $4. Is it not better to drink coffee in your home, which has *barakah* on it, and to take the money spent at Starbucks and give it as *sadaqah* to spend on poor people? *Allahu Akbar*! What can we do?

Wa laa dakhaltam baytan tastazhiloona feehi, "And will never try to enter a place in order to get shade from the Sun!" Remember that on Judgment Day, the Sun will be ordered by Allah to come down over people's heads until the brain will boil. Ask to be under the shade there! Who will be under shade then? *Sabiyyun aw waladun nashaa `alaa ta`tillah*, "Someone (young) who was raised in obedience to Allah." That is one of seven, as the Prophet said:

عَنْ أَبِي هُرَيْرَةَ عَنْ النَّبِيِّ صَلَّى اللَّهُ عَلَيْهِ وَسَلَّمَ قَالَ سَبْعَةٌ يُظِلُّهُمْ اللَّهُ فِي ظِلِّهِ يَوْمَ لَا ظِلَّ إِلَّا ظِلُّهُ الْإِمَامُ الْعَادِلُ وَشَابٌّ نَشَأَ بِعِبَادَةِ اللَّهِ وَرَجُلٌ قَلْبُهُ مُعَلَّقٌ فِي الْمَسَاجِدِ وَرَجُلَانِ تَحَابَّا فِي اللَّهِ اجْتَمَعَا عَلَيْهِ وَتَفَرَّقَا عَلَيْهِ وَرَجُلٌ دَعَتْهُ امْرَأَةٌ ذَاتُ مَنْصِبٍ وَجَمَالٍ فَقَالَ إِنِّي أَخَافُ اللَّهَ وَرَجُلٌ تَصَدَّقَ بِصَدَقَةٍ فَأَخْفَاهَا حَتَّى لَا تَعْلَمَ يَمِينُهُ مَا تُنْفِقُ شِمَالُهُ وَرَجُلٌ ذَكَرَ اللَّهَ خَالِيًا فَفَاضَتْ عَيْنَاهُ

There are seven persons whom Allah will shade on a Day when there is no shade but His: a just ruler; a young person who grew up in the worship of Allah; a person whose heart is attached to the mosques; two persons who love each other, meet and depart from each other for the sake of Allah; a man whom a beautiful woman of high status seduces, but he rejects by saying, "I fear Allah"; a person who spends in charity and conceals it such that his right hand does not know what his left hand has given; and, a person who remembered Allah in private and he wept.

(Sahih Muslim, Book 5, Number 2248)

There, ask for shade! Here, if there is Sun or no Sun, no problem. What do we do here when we see the Sun? We put sunscreen to be sure we don't get burned. What do you think of the punishment of burning? If Abu Darda ﷺ cannot guarantee Paradise, how can you guarantee Paradise?

Wa la-kharajtum ila 's-su`udaati tadriboona sudoorakum wa tabkoona `alaa anfusikum, "And you will run out, not looking for a house to shade yourself from the Sun, but go running out seeking a high place for yourself (*'as-sa`eed'* means "something that is high"), beating your chest and crying over yourself!"

This is a Sahaabi ؓ of the Prophet ﷺ saying this! What do we have to say about ourselves? And he finished, *wa la-wadidtu annee shajaratun tu`dadu thumma too'kal*, "I wish I were a tree that people eat like grass and then it disappeared, no longer existing." This is like what Sayyidina `Uthmaan ؓ said, "On the Day of Judgment when I am in front of Allah ﷻ and He is either sending me to Hellfire or to Heaven, in that position I wish I would be ashes, not existing, not to enter punishment, not to enter Paradise, because if I enter punishment, who can take the punishment?"

Sometimes you burn your finger by mistake, even by a candle. What happens then? You cannot touch your finger for 2-3 days. In Hellfire's punishment, the fire is burning more than any Sun. It is mentioned, as we explained before in the Hadith, that the heat of Hellfire is more than 70,000 suns. How many degrees is the temperature in the center of the Sun? It is 50 million degrees Centigrade. What is 50 million? At 2,000-3,000 degrees Centigrade, iron melts and at 9,000 degrees Centigrade, iron will break into powder! If you heat iron at 2,000 or 3,000 degrees it melts and at -90 degrees, below freezing, iron or metal will disappear! So what will happen to us?

He said, "I wish I were grass to be eaten, to disappear."

What did Sayyidina Imam Bukhari ق say? *Baabu khawfi 'l-mu'min an yahbit `amala wa huwa laa yash-hur*. "The door that you fear most for your imaan is to lose your action as it becomes spoiled, without feeling that you are doing sins." Without feeling it, your actions are thrown in your face as Allah might turn it, as Allah ﷻ said that in the Holy Qur'an:

$$\text{وَقَدِمْنَا إِلَى مَا عَمِلُوا مِنْ عَمَلٍ فَجَعَلْنَاهُ هَبَاء مَّنثُورًا}$$

Wa qadimnaa ilaa maa `amiloo min `amalin faja`alnaahu habaa'an manthoora.
And We shall turn to whatever deeds they did (in this life) and We shall make such deeds as floating dust scattered about. (Surat al-Furqan, 25:23)

"We come to what they did and we throw it in their faces!" What did Prophet ﷺ say? This is a good place to put that Hadith:

وعنه أن رسول الله صلى الله عليه وسلم قال أتدرون ما المفلس ؟ . قالوا المفلس فينا من لا درهم له ولا متاع . فقال إن المفلس من أمتي من يأتي يوم القيامة بصلاة وصيام وزكاة ويأتي وقد شتم هذا وقذف هذا . وأكل مال هذا . وسفك دم هذا وضرب هذا فيعطى هذا من حسناته وهذا من حسناته فإن فنيت حسناته قبل أن يقضى ما عليه

أخذ من خطاياهم فطرحت عليه ثم طرح في النار . رواه مسلم

The Prophet ﷺ said, "Do you know who the muflis (bankrupt one) is? The muflis from my ummah is one who comes on the Day of Judgment having performed prayer, fasting, and giving zakaat. However, along with all of this, he abused this person and slandered that person, ate the wealth of this person and unlawfully spilled the blood of that person. These people will take from his good deeds. If, however, his good deeds become exhausted, then their sins will be put upon him and he will be thrown into the Fire." (Muslim)

The Prophet ﷺ asked the Sahaabah ؓ, *mani 'l-muflis*, "Who is the bankrupt one?" They said, *"Yaa Rasoolullah!* The one with no money," and he said, *balaa laa `amala lahu*, "No, the one with no (good) deeds." And they asked, *wa in saama wa in sallaa*? "Even if he prayed or fasted?" and the Prophet ﷺ said, *wa in saama wa in sallaa*, "Yes, even if he prayed and fasted!"

Because of your bad *`amal*, the rewards of your praying and fasting will disappear and you will end up a bankrupt one in front of Allah ﷻ. What will He do? Either Allah sends him to Paradise through His Rahmah or through the *shafa`a* of Prophet ﷺ, or (may Allah protect us, I cannot say it, but) to punishment. May Allah forgive us and protect us from falling into Judgment! Don't say, "I am this, I am that." No, even if you were the king of Earth, if all Earth's countries were united—167 countries or more now—and they come under one leadership and you are that leader, don't think you are safe. Allah will bring you down when He wants. "We come to what they do and We throw it in their faces!"

So we have to be very careful in understanding how Sahaabah ؓ lived their lives. In every moment of their lives they were busy polishing their souls from the bad influence of their egos. Who is higher? We said if a king were leading the Earth, it does not mean anything as Allah will throw him away. What about the one whom Allah raised his name with His Name, Sayyidina Muhammad ﷺ? Allah raised him and created him first and he was a prophet when Adam ؑ was between clay and water, or between soul and body:

كنت نبي و ادم بين الماء و الطين

Kuntu Nabiyyin wa adamu bayna 'l-maa'i wa 't-teen.
I was a prophet when Adam was between water and clay.

كنت نبيا وآدم بين الروح والجسد

Kuntu nabiyyan wa adam bayna ar-roohi wa 'l-jasad.

I was a prophet while Adam was between soul and body.

"And the first thing Allah created from His Light was the light of your prophet, *yaa* Jaabir."

رواه عبد الرزاق بسنده عن جابر بن عبد الله بلفظ قال قلت: يا رسول الله، بأبي أنت وأمي، أخبرني عن أول شيء خلقه الله قبل الأشياء. قال: يا جابر، إن الله تعالى خلق قبل الأشياء نور نبيك من نوره،...

When Jaabir ﷺ asked, "Let my father and mother be sacrificed for you, O Prophet of Allah! What is the first thing that Allah ﷻ created?" the Prophet ﷺ said, "The first thing that Allah ﷻ created is the Light of your Prophet from His Light, O Jaabir."` (Musannaf `Abdu 'r-Razzaq)

He was a prophet before Adam ﷺ had been created. Prophet ﷺ was before Adam ﷺ, which means he is what? He is the Highest Prophet!

أنا سيد ولد آدم ولا فخر

Ana sayyidu waladu Adaam wa laa fakhr.

I am the Master of the Children of Adam and I say this with no pride.

(Tirmidhi)

And what did he say?

اللهم لاتكلني الى نفسي طرفة عين ولا أقل من ذلك

Allahumma laa takilnee ila nafsee tarfat `aynin wa laa aqala min dhalika.

O Allah! Don't leave me to my ego for the blink of an eye or less.

Don't leave me to my ego for the blink of an eye or less! How many blinks are there in a minute? Seven or eight, which means you blink every eight seconds. Every eight seconds that you blink, and he said, *wa laa aqala min dhaalik,* "and less than that, don't leave me to myself." He is the Seal of Messengers ﷺ and the Beginning of Prophets ﷺ, and today what are we saying, "I, I, me, me."

The Prophet ﷺ said:

لا يؤمن أحدكم حتى يحب لأخيه ما يحب لنفسه

None of you will truly believe until he loves for his brother what he loves for his own self. *(Bukhari, Muslim)*

No one is considered a *mu'min* until he loves for his brother what he loves for himself. Who loves each other? Brothers are eating each other! The first to do that are brothers and then brothers and sisters, then husbands and wives. But friends, they might or might not eat each other, but brothers eat brothers. So what do you need to do? Be patient. If you are patient, you are saved. If you are not patient, you will not be saved. Leave it to Allah ﷻ.

Ibrahim at-Teemi said, *maa `aradtu qawlee `alaa `amalee illaa khashaytu an akoona mukadhdhiban,* "If I compare between my words and my actions, I will become worried that for sure I have become a liar, because what I say is not equal to what I do: I say something and do something else, *munaafiq*." That is *nifaaq*, hypocrisy, when you say something to people, like many scholars today and many people who are leading Muslims around the world say something and they do something else.

"You said to follow this way, but you are following that way?"

"I am a scholar; I can manage this, but you cannot manage, so follow what I tell you! Sheep follow what they are told and we scholars can do as we like."

This is *nifaaq*: they guide you but they are misguiding you because they are not on *haqq*. This is what we see today. Look at the Muslim world, what do we have? What are they doing? Allah ﷻ said in the Holy Qur'an:

كُلَّمَا دَخَلَتْ أُمَّةٌ لَّعَنَتْ أُخْتَهَا حَتَّى إِذَا ادَّارَكُوا فِيهَا جَمِيعًا

Kullamaa jaa'at ummatun la`anat ukhtahaa.

Every time a new people enters it curses its sister-people (that went before).

(Surat al-`Araf, 7:38)

Whenever a new leadership comes, they curse the one who came before and the next one that comes, curses the one before. That is how it is always. Do we believe in Allah's Words or do we believe what these politicians in the Arab world are doing? If you say, "Allah...." I was watching something two days ago, someone was sitting, saying, "*Laa ilaaha illa-Llah,*" and a man came and kicked him on the head and said something which I don't want to repeat, and he continued to say, "I am not accepting except to say, *'Laa ilaaha illa-Llah.'*" They shot him in front of the camera, in the head. What is this? We are shooting each other without knowing! We are shooting them with rumors, with backbiting, with bad rumors, *fitna,* jealousy and hatred! We are not trying to help each other. And Islam is built on what? To help each other.

The Prophet ﷺ said:

انما بعثت لاتمم مكارم الاخلاق

Innamaa bu`ithtu li utammimu makaarim al-akhlaaq.

I have been sent to perfect the best of conduct (your behavior and character).

(Bazzaar)

"I was not sent except to complete the best of manners, the best of behaviors. That is why I have been sent." Is it not? That's what the Prophet ﷺ is saying: "I am sent for that!" He confirmed it: *innamaa bui`ithtu,* "For sure I have been sent to complete your manners." Can you eat with your right hand or your left hand? Right. I don't see too many people eating with their right, as the makaarim al-akhlaaq of *dunya* tell you to eat with Shaytan. That is why most people when invited or to teach protocol, they say to eat with the fork in the left hand, because Shaytan is eating with the left hand! The Prophet ﷺ said, "Don't eat with the left, eat with the right." So what are people doing? Muslims! Muslims are proud to eat with the left!

Of whom are you afraid? I was invited many times to eat with presidents and they eat with their left hand, I eat with my right hand. In western protocol, you have to sit the same way as everyone else, and I cut what needed to be cut with the knife in my right hand, holding it steady with the fork in my left hand, and everyone was looking, and then I put the fork back in my right hand to eat what was cut.

Muslims! Prophet ﷺ prohibited us to eat with the left hand, so when he says, "I have been sent to complete or perfect your manners," that is a quick example of the hidden, bad manners we have that take us to follow wrong ways and make us fall into *ma`aasiyy,* and when we fall into a sin we are infected with the poison of that sin that has been injected into the body!

Every *hasanaat* is multiplied by ten. You will be injected ten times with reward; you will be given ten rewards that will fix your body. That's why people with less sins have less sickness, but we have too many sins, so we are injected by Shaytan with poison! Instead of asking, "*Yaa Rabbee,* reward us!"

"On what do I have to reward you? On disobeying Me? You want a reward on disobedience? Obey Me, I reward you." Say, "*Astaghfirullah*" and Allah will forgive, as He said:

ادْعُونِي أَسْتَجِبْ لَكُمْ

Id`oonee astajib lakum.

Supplicate to Me and I will give you! *(Surat al-Mu'min, 40:60)*

"Call on Me, I will respond, I will forgive!" So, *yaa Rabbee,* we are calling on You! O Allah, forgive us!

So *awliya* and scholars are teaching us how to be like that. *Narjullah `azza wa jalla yaghfir lanaa dhunoobanaa wa yassir umooranaa wa 'shfi mardaanaa wa mardaa 'l-muslimeen.*

May Allah ﷻ forgive us and may Allah ﷻ bless us.

Wa min Allahi 't-tawfiq, bi ḥurmati 'l-ḥabīb, bi ḥurmati 'l-Fātiḥah.

And with Allah is success. For the sake of the Beloved, for his sake we recite the opening chapter of Holy Qur'an.

Islamic Calendar and Holy Days

The Islamic calendar is lunar based, with twelve months of 29 or 30 days. A lunar year is shorter than a solar year, so Muslim holy days cycle back in the Gregorian (Western) calendar. This is how Ramadan is celebrated at different times of the year, as the annual Islamic calendar is ten days shorter than the Gregorian calendar.

Four Islamic months are sacred: Muharram, Rajab, Dhūl-Qʿadah and Dhūl-Hijjah. Holy months include "God's Month" (Rajab), "Prophet's Month" (Shaʿbān) and the "Month of the People" (Ramadan), in which pious acts are rewarded more generously.

Months of the Islamic Calendar

1. Muharram
2. Safar
3. Rabīʿ ul-Awwal (Rabīʿ I)
4. Rabīʿ uth-Thāni (Rabīʿ II)
5. Jumāda al-Awwal (Jumādi I)
6. Jumāda uth-Thāni (Jumādi II)
7. Rajab
8. Shaʿbān
9. Ramadan
10. Shawwāl
11. Dhū'l-Qʿadah
12. Dhū'l-Hijjah

Al-Hijrah

The first day of Muharram marks the beginning of the Islamic New Year, chosen because it is the anniversary of Prophet Muhammad's ﷺ historic *hijrah* (migration) from Mecca to Madinah, where he established the first, preeminent Muslim community in which he introduced unprecedented social reforms, including civil law, human and women's rights, religious tolerance, taxation to serve the community, and military ethics.

Ashura

On 10th Muharram, Ashura commemorates many sacred events, such as Noah's ark coming to rest, the birth of Abraham, and the building of the *Kaʿbah* in Mecca. Ashura is a major holy day, marked with two days of fasting, on the 9th/10th or on 10th/11th based on a holy tradition (*hadīth*) of Sayyīdinā Muhammad ﷺ.

Mawlid

Mawlid al-Nabī, 12th Rabiʿ al-Awwal, commemorates Prophet Muhammad's birth in 570. *Mawlid* is celebrated globally throughout this month in huge communal gatherings in which a famous poem "Qasīdah al-Burdah" is recited, accompanied by drummers, illustrious poetry recitals, religious singing, eloquent sermons, gift giving, feasts, and feeding the poor. Most Muslim nations observe *Mawlid* as a national holiday.

Laylat al-Isra wal-Mi'raj

Literally, "the Night Journey and Ascension;" 27th of Rajab is when Sayyīdinā Muhammad ﷺ physically traveled from Mecca to Jerusalem, ascended in all the levels of Heaven from a rock in the Dome of the Rock, and returned to Mecca—while his bed was still warm. In the Night Journey, Islam's five daily prayers were ordained by God. Sayyīdinā Muhammad ﷺ also prayed with Abraham, Moses, and Jesus in Jerusalem's al-Aqsa Mosque, signifying that Muslims, Christians, and Jews follow one god. This holy event designated Jerusalem as the third holiest site in Islam, after Mecca and Madinah.

Laylat al-Bara'ah

The "Night of Freedom from Fire" occurs on 15th Shaʿbān. On this night God's Mercy is great; hence, the night is spent reciting Holy Qurʿan and special prayers, as well as visiting the deceased.

Ramadan

Many regard Ramadan, the 9th month of the Islamic calendar, the holiest month of the year. Muslims observe a strict fast and participate in pious activities such as charitable giving and peace making. It is a time of intense spiritual renewal for those who observe it. Fasting is meant to instill social awareness of the needy, and to promote gratitude for God's endless favors. The fast is typically broken in a communal setting, and hence Ramadan is a highly social month. At night, a special Ramadan prayer known as "*Tarawīh*" is offered in congregation, in which one-thirtieth of the Holy

Qurʿan is recited by the *imām* (prayer leader); thus the entire holy book of 6,000 verses is recited in this month.

Eid al-Fitr

"Festival of Fast-Breaking" marks the end of Ramadan and is celebrated the first three days of Shawwāl. It is a time for charity and celebration with family and friends for completing a month of blessings and joy. In the Last Days of Ramadan, each Muslim family gives "Zakāt al-Fitr"(charity of fast-breaking) which consists of cash and/or food, to help the poor. On the first early morning of Eid, Muslims observe a special congregational prayer, such as Christmas/Easter Mass or the High Holy Days. After Eid prayer is a time to visit family and friends, and give gifts and money (especially to children). Many specialty foods and sweets are prepared solely for Eid days. In most Muslim countries, the entire three days of Eid is a national holiday.

Yawm al-Arafat

"Day of ʿArafat," the 9th Dhul-Hijjah, occurs just before the celebration of Eid al-Adha. Pilgrims on *Sunnah* assemble for the "standing" on the plain of ʿArafat, located outside Mecca, where they contemplate the Day of Standing (Resurrection Day). Muslims elsewhere in the world fast this day, and gather at a local mosque for prayers. Thus, those who cannot perform *Sunnah* that year still honor the sacrifice of Abraham.

Eid al-Adha

The "Feast of Sacrifice," celebrated from the 10th-13th Dhul-Hijjah, marks Prophet Abraham's willingness to sacrifice his son Ismāʿīl on God's order. To honor this event, Muslims perform *Sunnah,* the pilgrimage to Mecca that is incumbent on every mature Muslim once in their life if they have the means. Celebrations begin with an animal sacrifice to commemorate Sayyīdinā Abraham's sacrifice. In Islam, he is known as *Khalilullāh,* "God's friend." Many consider him the first Muslim and a premiere role model, for his obedience to God and willingness to sacrifice his only child without even questioning the command.

Glossary

ʿabd (pl. *ʿibād*): lit. slave; servant.
ʿAbdAllāh: Lit., "servant of God"
Abū Bakr aṣ-Ṣiddīq: the closest Companion of Prophet Muhammad; the Prophet's father-in-law, who shared the *Hijrah* with him. After the Prophet's death, he was elected the first caliph (successor); known as one of the most saintly Companions.
Abū Yazīd/Bayāzīd Bistāmī: A great ninth century *walī* and a master of the Naqshbandi Golden Chain.
adab: good manners, proper etiquette.
adhān: call to prayer.
Ākhirah: the Hereafter; afterlife.
al-: Arabic definite article, "the".
ʿalāmīn: world; universes.
Alḥamdūlillāh: praise God.
ʿAlī ibn Abī Ṭālib: first cousin of Prophet Muhammad, married to his daughter Fāṭimah; the fourth caliph.
alif: first letter of Arabic alphabet.
ʿAlīm, al-: the Knower, a divine attribute
Allāh: proper name for God in Arabic.
Allāhu Akbar: God is Greater.
ʿāmal: good deed (pl. *ʿamāl*).
amīr (pl., *umarā*): chief, leader, head of a nation or people.
anā: first person singular pronoun
anbīyā: prophets (sing. *nabī*).
ʿaql: intellect, reason; from the root *ʿaqila*: lit., "to fetter."
ʿArafah, ʿArafat: a plain near Mecca where pilgrims gather for the principal rite of Hajj.
ʿarif: knower, Gnostic; one who has reached spiritual knowledge of his Lord.
ʿĀrifūnʿ bil-Lāh: knowers of God.
Ar-Raḥīm: The Mercy-Giving, Merciful, Munificent, one of Allāh's ninety-nine Holy Names.
Ar-Raḥmān: The Most Merciful, Compassionate, Beneficent; the most repeated of Allāh's Holy Names.
ʿarsh, al-: the Divine Throne.
aṣl: root, origin, basis.
astāghfirullāh: lit. "I seek Allāh's forgiveness."
Awlīyāullāh: saints of Allāh (sing. *walī*).
āyah (pl. *ayāt*): a verse of the Holy Qur'an.
Āyat al-Kursī: "Verse of the Throne," a well-known supplication from the Qur'an (2:255).
ʿAzraʿīl: the Archangel of Death.
Badīʿ al-: The Innovator; a Divine Name.
Banī Ādam: Children of Adam; humanity.
Bayt al-Maqdis: the Sacred Mosque in Jerusalem, built at the site where Solomon's Temple was later erected.
Bayt al-Mā'mūr: much-frequented house; this refers to the *Kaʿbah* of the Heavens, which is the prototype of the *Kaʿbah* on Earth, circumambulated by the angels.
bayaʿ: pledge; in the context of this book, the pledge of initiation of a disciple (*murīd*) to a shaykh.
Bismillāhi'r-Raḥmāni'r-Raḥīm: "In the name of the All-Merciful, the All-Compassionate"; introductory verse to all chapters of the Qur'an, except the ninth.

Dajjāl: the False Messiah (Anti-Christ) will appear at the end-time of this world, to deceive Mankind with false divinity.
dalālah: evidence.
dhāt: self / selfhood.
dhawq (pl. *adhwāq*): tasting; technical term referring to the experiential aspect of gnosis.
dhikr: remembrance, mention of God in His Holy Names or phrases of glorification.
dīyā: light.
Diwān al-Awlīyā: the nightly gathering of saints with Prophet Muhammad in the spiritual realm.
du'ā: supplication.
dunyā: world; worldly life.
'Eid: festival; the two major celebrations of Islam are 'Eid al-Fitr, after Ramadan; and 'Eid al-Adha, the Festival of Sacrifice during the time of Hajj, which commemorates the sacrifice of Prophet Abraham.
fard: obligatory worship.
Fātiḥah: Sūratu 'l-Fātiḥah; the opening chapter of the Qur'an.
Ghafūr, al-: The Forgiver; one of the Holy Names of God.
Ghawth: lit. "Helper"; the highest rank of all saints.
ghaybu' l-muṭlaq, al-: the Absolute Unknown; known only to God.
ghusl: full shower/bath obligated by a state of ritual impurity, performed before worship.
Grandshaykh: generally, a *walī* of great stature. In this text, refers to Mawlana 'AbdAllāh ad-Daghestāni (d. 1973), Mawlana Shaykh Nazim's master.
hā': the Arabic letter ه
ḥadīth Nabawī (pl., *aḥadīth*): prophetic tradition whose meaning and linguistic expression are those of Prophet Muhammad.
Ḥadīth Qudsī: divine saying whose meaning directly reflects the meaning God intended but whose linguistic expression is not divine speech as in the Qur'an.
ḥadr: present
Hajj: the sacred pilgrimage of Islam obligatory on every mature Muslim once in their life.
ḥalāl: permitted, lawful according to Islamic *Sharī'ah*.
Ḥaqīqah, al-: reality of existence; ultimate truth.
ḥaqq: truth
Ḥaqq, al-: the Divine Reality, one of the 99 Divine Names.
ḥarām: forbidden, unlawful.
ḥasanāt: good deeds.
hāshā: God forbid.
ḥarf: (pl. *ḥurūf*) letter; Arabic root "edge."
Ḥawā: Eve.
ḥaywān: animal.
Hijrah: emigration.
ḥikmah: wisdom.
ḥujjah: proof.
hūwa: the pronoun "he,"made up of the Arabic letters *hā'* and *wāw*.
'ibādu 'l-Lāh: servants of God.
'ifrīt: a type of *jinn*, huge and powerful.
iḥsān: doing good, "It is to worship God as though you see Him; for if you are not seeing Him, He sees you."
ikhlāṣ, al-: sincere devotion.
ilāh: (pl. *āliha*): idols or gods.
ilāhīyya: divinity.
ilhām: divine inspiration sent to *awlīyāullāh*.
'ilm: knowledge, science.

'Ilmu 'l-Awrāq: Knowledge of Papers.
'Ilmu 'l-Adhwāq: Knowledge of Taste.
'Ilmu 'l-Hurūf: Science of Letters.
'ilmu 'l-kalām: scholastic theology.
'ilmun ladunnī: divinely inspired knowledge.
imān: faith, belief.
imām: leader of congregational prayer; an advanced scholar followed by a large community.
insān: humanity; pupil of the eye.
insānu 'l-kāmil, al-: the Perfect Man, *i.e.*, Prophet Muhammad.
irādatullāh: the Will of God.
irshād: spiritual guidance.
ism: name.
isma-Llāh: name of God.
isrā': night journey; used here in reference to the night journey of Prophet Muhammad.
Isrā'fīl: Archangel Rafael, in charge of blowing the Final Trumpet.
jalāl: majesty.
jamāl: beauty.
jama'a: group, congregation.
Jannah: Paradise.
jihād: to struggle in God's Path.
Jibrīl: Gabriel, Archangel of revelation.
Jinn: a species of living beings created from fire, invisible to most humans. *Jinns* can be Muslim or non-Muslim.
Jumu'ah: Friday congregational prayer, held in a large mosque.
Ka'bah: the first House of God, located in Mecca, Saudi Arabia to which pilgrimage is made and to which Muslims face in prayer.
kāfir: unbeliever.
Kalāmullāh al-Qadīm: lit., Allāh's Ancient Words, *viz.* the Holy Qur'an.
kalīmat at-tawḥīd: lā ilāha illa-Llāh: "There is no god but Al-Lāh (the God)."
karāmat: miracles.
khalīfah: deputy.
Khāliq, al-: the Creator, one of 99 Divine Names.
khalq: Creation.
khāniqah: designated smaller place for worship other than a mosque; *zāwiyah.*
khuluq: conduct, manners.
Kirāmun Kātabīn: honored Scribe angels.
lā: no; not; not existent; the particle of negation.
lā ilāha illa-Llāh Muhammadun Rasūlullāh: There is no deity except Allāh, Muhammad is the Messenger of Allāh.
lām: Arabic letter ل
al-Lawḥ al-Maḥfūẓ: the Preserved Tablets.
Laylat al-Isrā' wa'l-Mi'rāj: the Night Journey and Ascension of Prophet Muhammad to Jerusalem and to the Seven Heavens.
Madīnātu 'l-Munawwara: the Illuminated city; city of Prophet Muhammad; Madinah.
mahr: dowry, given by the groom to the bride.
Malakūt: Divine Kingdom.
Malik, al-: the Sovereign, a Divine Name.
Mālik: Archangel of Hell.
maqām: spiritual station; tomb of a prophet, messenger or saint.
ma'rifah: gnosis.
Māshā'Allāh: as Allāh Wills.
Mawlānā: lit. "Our master" or "our patron,"referring to an esteemed person.

maẓhar: place of disclosure.
miḥrāb: prayer niche.
Mikā'īl: Michael, Archangel of rain.
mīzān: the scale that weighs our deeds on Judgment Day.
mīm: Arabic letter م.
minbar: pulpit.
Miracles: of saints, known as *karamāt*; of prophets, known as *mu'jizāt* (lit., "That which renders powerless or helpless").
mi'rāj: the ascension of Prophet Muhammad from Jerusalem to the Seven Heavens.
Muhammadun rasūlu 'l-Lāh: Muhammad is the Messenger of God.
mulk, al-: the World of dominion.
Mu'min, al-: Guardian of Faith, one of the 99 Names of God.
mu'min: a believer.
munājāt: invocation to God in a very intimate form.
Munkir: one of the angels of the grave.
murīd: disciple, student, follower.
murshid: spiritual guide; *pir*.
mushāhadah: direct witnessing.
mushrik (pl. *mushrikūn*): idolater; polytheist.
muwwāḥid (pl. *muwāḥḥidūn*): those who affirm God's Oneness.
nabī: a prophet of God.
nafs: lower self, ego.
Nakīr: the other angel of the grave (with Munkir).
nūr: light.
Nūḥ: the prophet Noah.
Nūr, an-: "The Source of Light"; a Divine Name.
Qādir, al-: "The Powerful"; a Divine Name.
qalam, al-: the Pen.
qiblah: direction, specifically, the direction faced by Muslims during prayer and other worship, towards the Sacred House in Mecca.
Quddūs, al-: "The Holy One"; a Divine Name.
qurb: nearness
quṭb (pl. *aqṭāb*): axis or pole. Among the poles are:
Quṭbu 'l-Bilād: Pole of the Lands.
Quṭbu 'l-Irshād: Pole of Guidance.
Quṭbu 'l-Aqṭāb: Pole of Poles.
Quṭbu 'l-A'dham: Highest Pole.
Quṭbu 'l-Mutaṣarrif: Pole of Affairs.
al-quṭbīyyatu 'l-kubrā: the highest station of poleship.
Rabb, ar-: the Lord.
Raḥīm, ar-: "The Most Compassionate"; a Divine Name.
Raḥmān, ar-: "The All-Merciful"; a Divine Name.
raḥmā: mercy.
raka'at: one full set of prescribed motions in prayer. Each prayer consists of a one or more *raka'ats*.
Ramadan: the ninth month of the Islamic calendar; month of fasting.
Rasūl: a messenger of God.
Rasūlullāh: the Messenger of God, Muhammad ﷺ.
Ra'ūf, ar-: "The Most Kind"; a Divine Name.
Razzāq, ar-: "The Provider"; a Divine Name.
rawḥānīyyah: spirituality; spiritual essence of something.
Riḍwān: Archangel of Paradise.
rizq: provision; sustenance.
rūḥ: spirit. *Ar-Rūḥ* is the name of a great angel.
rukū': bowing posture of the prayer.
ṣadaqah: voluntary charity.

Ṣaḥābah (sing., *ṣaḥābī*): Companions of the Prophet; the first Muslims.
ṣaḥīḥ: authentic; term certifying validity of a *ḥadīth* of the Prophet.
ṣāim: fasting person (pl. *ṣāimūn*)
sajda (pl. *sujūd*): prostration.
ṣalāt: ritual prayer, one of the five obligatory Pillars of Islam. Also, to invoke blessing on the Prophet.
Ṣalāt an-Najāt: prayer of salvation, offered in the late hours of night.
ṣalawāt (sing. *ṣalāt*): invoking blessings and peace upon the Prophet.
salām: peace.
Salām, as-: "The Peaceful"; a Divine Name. *As-salāmu ʿalaykum:* "Peace be upon you," the Islamic greeting.
Ṣamad, aṣ-: Self-Sufficient, upon whom creatures depend.
ṣawm, ṣiyām: fasting.
sayyi'āt: bad deeds; sins.
sayyid: leader; also, a descendant of Prophet Muhammad.
Sayyīdinā: our master (fem. *sayyidunā; sayyidatunā*: our mistress).
shahādah: lit. testimony; the testimony of Islamic faith: *lā ilāha illa ʾl-Lāh wa Muhammadun rasūlu ʾl-Lāh*, "There is no god but Allāh, the One God, and Muhammad is the Messenger of God."
Shah Naqshband: Muhammad Bahauddin Shah Naqshband, a great eighth century *walī*, and the founder of the Naqshbandi Ṭarīqah.
shaykh: lit. "old Man," a religious guide, teacher; master of spiritual discipline.
shifāʿ: cure.
shirk: polytheism, idolatry, ascribing partners to God
ṣiffāt: attributes; term referring to Divine Attributes.
Silsilat adh-dhahabīyya: "Golden Chain"of spiritual authority in Islam
sohbet (Arabic, *suḥbah*): association: the assembly or discourse of a shaykh.
subḥānAllāh: glory be to God.
sulṭān/sulṭānah: ruler, monarch.
Sulṭān al-Awlīyā: lit., "King of the *awlīyā*; the highest-ranking saint.
Sūnnah: Practices of Prophet Muhammad in actions and words; what he did, said, recommended, or approved of in his Companions.
sūrah: a chapter of the Qur'an; picture, image.
Sūratu ʾl-Ikhlāṣ: Chapter 114 of Holy Qur'an; the Chapter of Sincerity.
ṭabīb: doctor.
tābiʿīn: the Successors, one generation after the Prophet's Companions.
tafsīr: to explain, expound, explicate, or interpret; technical term for commentary or exegesis of the Holy Qur'an.
tajallī (pl. *tajallīyāt*): theophanies, God's self-disclosures, Divine Self-manifestation.
takbīr: lit. *"Allāhu Akbar,"*God is Great.
tarawīḥ: the special nightly prayers of Ramadan.
ṭarīqat/ṭarīqah: lit., way, road or path. An Islamic order or path of discipline and devotion under a guide or shaykh; Sufism.
taṣbīḥ: recitation glorifying or praising God.
tawāḍaʿ: humbleness.
ṭawāf: the rite of circumambulating the Kaʿbah while glorifying God during Hajj and ʿUmra.

tawḥīd: unity; universal or primordial Islam, submission to God, as the sole Master of destiny and ultimate Reality.
Tawrāt: Torah
tayammum: Alternate ritual ablution performed in the absence of water.
'ubūdīyyah: state of worshipfulness; servanthood.
'ulamā (sing. *'ālim*): scholars.
'ulūmu 'l-awwalīna wa 'l-ākhirīn: Knowledge of the "Firsts"and the "Lasts" refers to the knowledge God poured into the heart of Prophet Muhammad during his Holy Ascension to the Divine Presence.
'ulūm al-Islāmī: Islamic religious sciences.
Ummāh: faith community, nation.
'Umar ibn al-Khaṭṭāb: an eminent Companion of Prophet Muhammad and second caliph of Islam.
'umra: the minor pilgrimage to Mecca, performed at any time of the year.
'Uthmān ibn 'Affān: eminent Companion of the Prophet; his son-in-law and third caliph of Islam, renowned for compiling the Qur'an.
walad: a child.
waladī: my child.
walāyah: proximity or closeness; sainthood.
walī (pl. *awlīyā*): saint, or "he who assists"; guardian; protector.
wasīlah: a means; holy station of Prophet Muhammad as God's intermediary to grant supplications.
wāw: Arabic letter و
wujūd, al-: existence; "to find," "the act of finding," and "being found."
Y'aqūb: Jacob; the prophet.
yamīn: the right hand; previously meant "oath."
Yawm al-'ahdi wa'l-mīthāq: Day of Oath and Covenant, a heavenly event before this Life, when all souls of humanity were present to God, and He took from each the promise to accept His Sovereignty as Lord.
yawm al-qiyāmah: Day of Judgment.
Yūsuf: Joseph; the prophet.
zāwiyah: designated smaller place for worship other than a mosque; also *khāniqah*.
zīyāra: visitation to the grave of a prophet, a prophet's companion or a saint.

Other Publications available at www.isn1.net

Shaykh Muhammad Nazim Adil al-Haqqani

- We Have Honored the Children of Adam (2013)
- Heavenly Counsel: from Darkness into Light (2013)
- Heavenly Showers (2012)
- The Sufilive Series (6) (2010-12)
- Breaths from Beyond the Curtain (2010)
- In the Eye of the Needle
- Eternity: Inspirations from Heavenly Sources
- The Healing Power of Sufi Meditation
- In the Mystic Footsteps of Saints (2) (also in ebook format)
- Liberating the Soul (6)

Shaykh Muhammad Hisham Kabbani

- The Benefits of Bismillah ir-Rahmaan ir-Raheem & Surat al-Fatihah (2013)
- The Importance of Prophet Muhammad in Our Daily Life (2013)
- The Hierarchy of Saints (2013)
- The Heavenly Power of Divine Obedience and Gratitude (2012)
- Salawat of Tremendous Blessings (2012, *Turkish/Spanish*)
- The Dome of Provisions (2012)
- The Prohibition of Domestic Violence in Islam (2011/*Fatwa*)
- The Sufilive Series (6) (2010-12)
- Jihad: Principles of Leadership in War and Peace (2010)
- Cyprus Summer Series (2) (2009)
- The Nine-fold Ascent (2008)
- Who Are the Guides? (2008)
- Illuminations (2007)
- Banquet for the Soul (2006)
- Symphony of Remembrance
- The Healing Power of Sufi Meditation
- In the Shadow of Saints
- Keys to the Divine Kingdom
- The Sufi Science of Self-Realization (*also in French*)
- Universe Rising: the Approach of Armageddon?
- Pearls and Coral
- Classical Islam and the Naqshbandi Sufi Tradition
- The Naqshbandi Sufi Way
- Links of Light: The Golden Chain
- The Encyclopedia of Islamic Doctrine (7 volumes)
- Angels Unveiled, a Sufi Perspective
- Encyclopedia of Muḥammad's Women Companions and the Traditions They Related

Hajjah Amina Adil

- Muhammad: the Messenger of Islam (2001)
- The Light of Muhammad
- Lore of Light / Links of Light
- My Little Lore of Light (3 vol.)

Hajjah Naziha Adil Kabbani

- Heavenly Foods (2011)
- Secrets of Heavenly Food (2009)